LANGUAGE PROCESS NOTES

USING WORDS TO GET BEYOND WORDS

Harbert Rice

Language Process Notes
Using Words To Get Beyond Words
by Harbert Rice

Copyright © 2008 by Harbert Rice

All rights reserved. Please address reproduction requests to:
    Harbert Rice
    Reno, NV
    hvrice@gmail.com

Distributed by The Focusing Institute. Please address all copy requests to:
    The Focusing Institute
    Spring Valley, NY
    info@focusing.org
    www.focusing.org

Library of Congress Control Number: 2008902198

ISBN: 978-0-9816186-0-9

Printed in the United States of America
0 9 8 7 6 5 4 3 2 1

Cover and Page Design by One-On-One Book Production, West Hills, CA.

For my wife Becky.

Table of Contents

1. Introduction — 1
2. Three Practices — 5
3. Understanding Symbol Space — 19
4. Living in Symbol Space — 41
5. Change and Transformation — 51

References — 103

Appendix A: Light Meditation — 107

Appendix B: Five Steps in TAE — 109

Index — 115

About the Author — 119

1. Introduction

Last spring I realized that I spoke three languages. I realized that I could seek and experience personal change by engaging in language arising from Quaker, Focusing, and Nonviolent Communication (NVC) practices. My own practice is Quaker, but each practice has given me some understanding of how I may choose to speak and to live my life in a more caring and loving way. I care for my friends from each of these practices, and I want them to speak more with one another. Responding to this wanting, I felt led to pull together these Notes, which I am calling "Language Process Notes."

Using Words to Get Beyond Words

These Notes draw upon the experiential philosophy of Gene Gendlin. The Notes make use of both the concepts and the conceptualization process given by Gendlin in *A Process Model*.[1]

"Language Process" refers to an understanding of language in relation to felt experiencing, which lets us see Quaker, Focusing and NVC practices as "using words in order to get beyond words" to change and transform our lives, and "to speak (use) words in a new way."

Section 2. Three Practices introduces this theme of "using words to get beyond words" in terms of the inner movement for personal change sought in each practice. *Section 3. Symbol Space* provides a primer on Gendlin's philosophy. Symbol space is the environment, which we have created with our use of language. *Section 4. Living in Symbol Space* describes how our modern living both hinders and compels us to seek change. *Section 5. Change and Transformation* contains my Quaker Meditations on how we change and transform our lives, and explores my experiences with each practice.

---

[1] E. Gendlin, 1997, *A Process Model*, abbreviated as APM in the following footnotes.

Suggestions on How to Read These Notes

One early reader (Mary Hendricks) suggested these Notes are really a "little book," a little book of philosophy. If you are familiar with Gendlin's philosophy and *A Process Model*, you likely will be able to read the Notes straight through. If you are coming upon this philosophy for the first time, then you may find *Section 3. Symbol Space* a dense and difficult read. Not only are the concepts different from our usual observer's view of the world, they also require a *different way of thinking*. For example, the model language process used here is upside down to the way we usually think about language[2] – we say words "come to us" from a felt experiencing of meaning, rather than saying we get meaning from words "representing" our experiences. If this philosophy is new to you, I suggest you first read through *Section 3.* without trying to master each concept; you can always come back for a second longer look at the concepts later. The process concepts are based on felt sensing. My own experience is that it takes some time to "settle in" and get comfortable with the basic concepts and the conceptualization process. As you read through *Section 3.*, try, if you can, to get a felt sense of "Symbolizing Meaning," "How Words Work," and "Metaphor" from your own experiences in using language.

Section 4. Living in Symbol Space offers a reading respite after working through the concepts in *Section 3*. The last section in the Notes, *Section 5. Change and Transformation*, uses and builds upon the language concepts from *Symbol Space*, and introduces the concept of *Implicit Space*. Implicit space is a new environment, which we create when we seek to "meet" a situation. Interacting in implicit space lets us "get beyond words" to encounter life in a new way that leads to change and transformation. This section contains my work on experientially "crossing" Quaker, Focusing, and NVC practices, and shows how each practice may enhance the others in helping us seek change. I suggest you read this last section by testing the concepts against your own life experiences, seeing if what I say "fits" your own felt experiencing of personal change.

---

[2] Gendlin suggests, I think rightly, that we are finally getting our language process right side up.

Intent and Hope

In putting out these Notes, I intend to foster an understanding of what I see as an underlying language process common to each practice leading to change and transformation. In turn, I hope that this understanding will help us to draw upon one another's insights, and lead us to wider and deeper peaceful ways of living in this world. While these Notes draw upon Quaker, Focusing, and NVC practices, the underlying language process is open to anyone who seeks change and transformation in his or her life.

2. Three Practices

Let's begin by looking at Quaker, Nonviolent Communication (NVC), and Focusing practices.

Where We Are Now

It has been more than 350 years since George Fox and a band of Quakers set out from the hills of Yorkshire in England to claim a new way of living. They called themselves "Friends of Truth" and set out a practice of seeking what they called the "inward light." We have only the barest instructions for this practice from Fox and the early Quakers. For example, consider the following instruction:

> Be still and cool in your own mind and spirit from your own thoughts, and you will then feel the divine source of life in you turn your mind to the Lord God. And in doing this you will receive his strength and life-giving power to quieten every storm and gale which blows against you... When the light discloses and reveals things to you, things that tempt you, that confuse you, distract you and the like, don't go looking at them, but look at the light that has made you aware of them. And with this same light you will feel yourself rising above them and empowered to resist them... That enables you to overcome them, and you will find grace and strength. And there is the first step to peace.[1]

Fox and the first generation of Quakers sought to transform the world. While failing in this first attempt to create a "New Eden," Quakers have settled in for the long haul of living and making peace in

---

[1] George Fox translated into Modern English (TME) in R. Ambler, 2002, *Light to live by*, p.20.

this violent world.[2] We attend our meetings, sitting in silence, minding the inward light, seeking guidance and drawing strength to live out what we call "testimonies," our outward practices of simplicity, peace, integrity, community, and equality. Unless they have had direct contact with a Quaker or a Quaker service organization, people often are surprised to find that we Quakers still exist, thinking (I am guessing) that we had been relegated long ago to just appearing as a picture on cardboard boxes of "Quaker Oats." Occasionally, one of our members will step forth to rivet our attention and the world's attention on what peace means. In my own time, I am thinking (as I write this) of the Quaker Norman Morrison who in 1965 immolated himself on the steps of the Pentagon to protest our government's actions in the Viet Nam War.[3]

In beginning her account of Norman Morrison's death, his wife Anne quotes the line:

> It is the sobering truth that only with the greatest difficulty can we convey our life, our meaning, to other people.[4]

This thought squares with the Quaker understanding that we cannot convey the meaning of our lives with words alone. In order to come to peace within ourselves and to create peace in the world, we must somehow get to a place beyond words. We must "let our lives speak." For Norman Morrison, getting to this place led him to take the suffering of others on to himself, and he could, in the end, only point to his meaning in this terrible way.

I do not mean to imply that getting to a place beyond words leads us to step beyond living and cease to speak; letting "our lives speak" does

---

[2] Quakers are called Quakers because many early Quakers would tremble and quake when they spoke in their Meetings. Many modern Quakers still tremble with the experience of speaking "out of the silence."

[3] For a narrative of Norman Morrison's action, please see Anne Morrison Welsh, 2005, *Fire of the Heart*, Pendle Hill Pamphlet #381, Pendle Hill Publications, Wallingford, PA.

[4] Ibid., p. 3.

not mean not speaking. What Quakers mean is that we must speak in a different manner, in a new way. Fox in a letter to Quakers says,

> Be patient as much as you need to be, and let everything you say be seasoned with grace, so that it edifies people. And by speaking in this way you will season the earth, your own hearts being established in the process, and you will be free of unsavoury ways of speaking, and unsavoury speakers, and you will live in the truth beyond their reach.[5]

Notions

While all Quakers are not led to self-sacrifice like Norman Morrison, we still must confront the difficulty of getting to that place beyond words. What keeps us then from getting to that place? Why is "turning to the light" so hard?

Again, Fox provides us with some guidance:

> So long as you live in the light nothing can trip you up, because you will see everything in the light. Do you love the light? Then here's your teacher! When you are walking it's there with you, in your heart – you don't have to say 'Look over here,' 'Look over there.' And as you lie in bed it is there with you too, teaching you, making you aware of that wandering mind of yours that likes to wander off, and of your attempts to master everything with your own thought and imagination – they themselves are mastered by the light. For if you follow your own thoughts you will soon get lost. But if you live in this light it will reveal to you the root of your wrong-doing, and the distortions of your life, and the degraded condition in which you live, and your endless thinking about everything.[6]

---

[5] George Fox in R. Ambler, 2001, *Truth of the Heart*, pp. 109-111.
[6] George Fox in R. Ambler, 2002, Op. cit., p. 8.

Following Fox, we come to see our own thinking mind blocks our way forward, or in a word from those times – our "notions" – our own ideas, concepts and imaginings stand in our way. The light then is our inner capacity to see, to separate out our own thinking from the truth. And what is this truth? Expressed in modern terms, it is the reality of our lives, our experiences without the stories we tell ourselves or tell others about ourselves. We learn the truth about ourselves:[7]

> For with the light man sees himself.[8]

Nonviolent Communication

Now, if we turn to look at Nonviolent Communication (NVC), a contemporary process developed by Marshall Rosenberg to speak and act in a nonviolent way, we can see a similar arc of expressions. In his book laying out NVC, Marshall starts by saying,

> Believing it is our nature to enjoy giving and receiving in a compassionate manner, I have been preoccupied most of my life with two questions: What happens to disconnect us from our compassionate nature, leading us to behave violently and exploitatively? And conversely, what allows some people to stay connected to their compassionate nature under even the most trying of circumstances?[9]
>
> While studying the factors that affect our ability to stay compassionate, I was struck by the crucial role of language and our use of words. I have since identified a specific approach to communicating – speaking and listening – that leads us to give from the heart, connecting us with ourselves and with each other in a way that allows our natural compassion to flourish. I call this approach Nonviolent Communication [NVC], using the

---

[7] See R. Ambler, 2001, Op. cit., pp. 176-200.

[8] Ibid., p. 32.

[9] Marshall Rosenberg, 2003, *Nonviolent Communication*, p. 1.

term *nonviolence* as Gandhi used it – to refer to our natural state of compassion when violence has subsided from the heart.[10]

Marshall then explains that NVC is way of focusing our attention:

> NVC guides us in reframing how we express ourselves and hear others. Instead of habitual, automatic reactions, our words become conscious responses based firmly on our awareness of what we are perceiving, feeling, and wanting… We learn to identify and clearly articulate what we are concretely wanting in a given situation… When we focus on clarifying what is being observed, felt, and needed rather than diagnosing and judging, we discover the depth of our own compassion.[11]

But, Marshall makes clear that he is talking about more than just language and process:

> Although I refer to it as a 'process of communication' or a 'language of compassion,' NVC is more than a process or a language. On a deeper level, it is an on-going reminder to keep our attention focused on a place where we are more likely to get what we are seeking.[12]

And

> The essence of NVC is to be found in our consciousness… not in the actual words exchanged.[13]

Jackal Talk

So, like Quakers, Marshall suggests that we seek a place, or a consciousness, which lets us use words in a different way. He then asks and answers the question of what blocks this natural flow of compassion:

---

[10] Ibid., p. 2.
[11] Ibid., pp. 3-4.
[12] Ibid., p. 4.
[13] Ibid., p. 8.

It is our nature to enjoy giving and receiving compassionately. We have, however, learned many forms of 'life-alienating communication' that lead us to speak and behave in ways that injure others and ourselves. One form of life-alienating communication is the use of moralistic judgments that imply wrongness or badness on the part of those who don't act in harmony with our values. Another form of such communication is the use of comparisons, which can block compassion for others and ourselves. Life-alienating communication also obscures our awareness that we are each responsible for our own thoughts, feelings, and actions. Communicating our desires in the form of demands is yet another characteristic of language that blocks compassion.[14]

In workshops, Marshall and his co-workers often refer to these collected blocks as "Jackal Talk" or "Jackal Thinking." The "Jackal" comes from Marshall's use of a jackal puppet to express the mind flow of these judgments, comparisons, and demands as they arise in dialogue.[15] Like Quakers, NVC as a practice suggests that blocks to our compassion come from our thinking patterns and learned expressions. Practice using the "light of consciousness" will get us past these blocks and let us speak in a new way.

Understanding Language

In the process leading up to setting out these Notes, I realized that I really did not understand, in any meaningful way, how language works. I have used words my whole life. I love words. But, if you think about it, what we Quakers (and Marshall) are saying is:

"We are going to use words to learn to get beyond words in order to speak (use) words in a new way."

How is that possible?

---

[14] Ibid., pp. 23-24.

[15] Marshall uses a giraffe puppet to model NVC dialogue responses and expressions. NVC "consciousness" often is called "giraffe consciousness."

I have always had a vague, common sense notion that words are unit symbols that represent the world in some way. We conceptualize our experience of the world by stringing words together with some set of rules or relationships. The meaning of each word is understood because the meanings are commonly shared. (If I am uncertain about a meaning, I can look the word up in the dictionary – or just ask a knowledgeable friend).

The rules of relationships are shared, or at least understood in the same way. I learned some of the rules in school, but I already knew most of the rules anyway by just *growing up* with the language. (Although to this day I still can't get it straight when to use *which* and when to use *that* in a sentence.) So, when I express myself, I put these word strings together and am confident that I will be understood more often than not.

Looking back, the whole language process seemed pretty straightforward. This common sense view, I realize now, is an "objective" view of language. I imagine that this view is quite useful if we are collecting the common usage of words, or seeking to see how a grammar is changing. However, when we look at language in this way we become "observers." We drop "ourselves" out of the process. We do not *experience* our use of language in this common sense way. If we examine language as if it were an arm's length experiment, we lose sight of the fact that we are *participants* in the experiment. To gain some understanding of how Quaker (and NVC) practices might work as language processes, we need a better understanding of how we actually experience and use language. We need to understand language from a process point of view. To gain this point of view, I want to turn to the work of Gene Gendlin.

Focusing

I want to begin by talking about Gene Gendlin's work developing the practice called *Focusing*.[16] Gendlin developed Focusing out of psychotherapy work that he did with Carl Rodgers at the University of Chicago in the early 1950's.[17] Trained in philosophy, Gendlin was

---

[16] E. Gendlin, 1981, *Focusing*.

[17] C. Purton, 2004, describes the origins of Focusing in *Person-Centred Therapy*, pp. 54-81. Marshall Rosenberg also studied with Carl Rodgers.

interested in the question of how we conceptualize and speak about our experience. What drew Gendlin to join Rodgers' counseling center was the fact that Rodgers and his co-workers were letting patients experience and express their therapy in a non-directive way. Patients were attending to their own attempts at healing, and expressing their process and progress in their sessions with therapists. The therapists provided empathy, listening, and reflection to support the patients.

In his *Focusing* book, Gendlin describes this work:[18]

> At the University of Chicago and elsewhere ... a group of colleagues and I have been studying some questions that most psychotherapists don't like to ask out loud. Why doesn't therapy succeed more often? Why does it often fail to make a real difference in people's lives? In the rarer cases when it does succeed, what is it that those patients and therapists do? What is it that the majority fail to do?
>
> Seeking answers, we studied many forms of therapy from classical approaches to recent ones. We analyzed literally thousands of therapist-patient sessions recorded on tape. Our series of studies has led to several findings, some very different from what we and most other professional therapists expected.
>
> First, we found that the successful patient – the one who shows real and tangible change on psychological tests and in life – can be picked out fairly readily from recorded therapy sessions. What these rare patients do in their therapy hours is different from the others...
>
> What is the crucial difference? We found that it is not the therapist's technique – differences in methods of therapy mean surprisingly little. Nor does the difference lie in what the patients talk about. The difference is in *how* they talk. And that is only an outward sign of the real difference: *what the successful patients do inside themselves*.

---

[18] E. Gendlin, 1981, Op. cit., pp. 3-4.

Inner Movement

What did Gendlin see? He saw what he came to call an "inner act" or an "inner movement." These "rare" patients turned their attention inward and seemed to connect with an inner bodily awareness of their life situation. Once this connection was made, change became possible. Gendlin calls this bodily awareness a *felt sense*.[19] When we turn our attention inward, it takes some time for a felt sense to form:

> A felt sense is usually not just there, it must form. You have to let it form by attending inside your body. When it comes, it is at first unclear, fuzzy…it can come into focus and change. A felt sense is the body's sense of a particular problem or situation… It feels meaningful, but not known. It is a body-sense of meaning.[20]

While attending to the felt sense is a *feeling* process, Gendlin makes it quite clear that the felt sense is different than an emotion:

> An emotion is often sharp and clearly felt, and often comes with a handy label by which you can describe it: "anger," "fear," "love" and so on. A felt sense, being larger and more complicated, is almost always unclear – at least until you focus on it – and almost never comes with a convenient label. [21]

As a felt sense emerges and you focus on it, you can begin to describe it. Words or images will come to you to express what you are feeling. These words feel fresh and usually come in descriptive bunches as the felt sense opens up. The initial feeling of vagueness gives way to more detail as your concern or problem emerges. Often what comes is a surprise, "Oh, it's about *that*!" Where *that* is a problem or a situation you had set aside or consciously avoided. Or, *that* may be a markedly different point of view on a problem you have focused on. As the felt sense forms, you usually can find a word, phrase, or image that resonates with it, that "fits" it. When you find some expression or image that fits,

---

[19] Ibid., p. 10.
[20] Ibid., p. 10.
[21] Ibid., p. 35.

you experience the felt sense more directly – as if you were sitting with a not-yet-clear meaning and direction. At some point, you often will experience a bodily sense of relief, a total relaxation as you get a sense of solution, of meaning and direction to your situation. This sense of solution may come directly, or it may come in response to a question like "What do I need to know?" Gendlin calls this bodily sensing of solution a *felt shift*.[22] You have a sense of solution to the *whole* situation. The immediate steps you need to take to resolve your problem or situation may not be clear, but where you were hopelessly "stuck" before, you have a sense of coming "unstuck." You have changed and your sense of your situation has changed. You can "get on" with your life and "meet" the situation.

Focusing as a Skill

In order to make this inner movement more accessible, Gendlin put together a set of six steps,[23] so that he and his co-workers could teach the process as a skill. Focusing skills now are taught and used as an adjunct in psychotherapy.[24] Using Focusing in this way is more popular in Europe, especially among those therapists using person-centered therapies, than in the US where cognitive therapies have held wider sway. However, Focusing is not confined to use in psychotherapy. Within the US, Europe, and elsewhere, Focusing skills also are taught and used as means of self-help and self-healing.[25]

Blocks to Focusing

While we can learn to use and practice Focusing, it still is not easy. As in Quaker practice and NVC, we easily encounter ways of approaching a problem or a situation that don't work. Again, these are things that we

---

[22] Ibid., p. 39.

[23] Ibid., pp. 42-45. The six steps are: (1) clearing a space, (2) felt sense, (3) handle, (4) resonating, (5) asking, and (6) receiving. We will look at these steps later in more detail.

[24] C. Purton, 2004, Op. cit., pp. 82-95.

[25] There is a certification process for both therapists and non-therapists to learn and to teach Focusing. For more information, see focusing.org.

think and tell ourselves to say or do. Gendlin lists some of the more common approaches that don't work:[26]

Belittling the problem. You try to convince yourself that the problem doesn't exist or is too trivial to worry about.

Analyzing... The analysis may or not be correct. But it does nothing to change the feeling [of discomfort]... You can analyze furiously, but [the situation] will not be eased anymore than it was last time.

Facing down the feeling... 'I'll ignore it. I won't let it get to me.' ... If something gets you, it will go on getting you until some fundamental change takes place.

Lecturing yourself. 'Now see here,' you tell yourself sternly, 'it's time you pulled yourself together and stopped all this nonsense. You're supposed to be an adult, right? So act like one!'

Drowning in the feeling. You sink into the emotion, hoping that this time just feeling it again will change it... Whenever you sink into this unchanged feeling, it makes you feel as bad as it did last time.

As Gendlin comments,

These approaches cannot work because they don't touch and change the place out of which the discomfort [of a situation] arises. It exists in the body. It is physical. If you want to change it, you must introduce a process of change that is also physical.[27]

---

[26] E. Gendlin, 1981, Op. cit., pp. 36-37.
[27] Ibid., p. 37.

What Have We Gained?

What have we gained by looking at Gendlin's Focusing? Like Quaker practice and NVC, Focusing can bring change to our lives, taking us to a place beyond words:

> When you look for a felt sense, you look in the place you know without words, in body-sensing. [28]

In Focusing, however, we clearly are working with a bodily process. The identifiable keys to this inner bodily process are:

Felt Sense. This underlying change process is a feeling process attending to experience. When engaged, the felt sense is both vague and intricate at the same time. It implicitly provides both meaning and direction in changing a life situation.

Symbolizing. We encounter a felt meaning when we interact with a felt sense by trying to find a word or an image that fits it. This interaction makes the meaning and direction of the felt sense immediate, concrete, and explicit. If you Focus, or sit with someone who is Focusing, you have a sense of words coming more directly, less bound or masked by social conventions. It was this element of observing how people express themselves that first drew Gendlin's attention.

Felt Shift. When the felt meaning becomes explicit, we often experience a felt shift – a sense of relief. This experience provides a sense both of an unfolding and of being "pulled along" and "led" by our participation in an unfolding process. Again, if you sit with someone who is Focusing and experiencing a felt shift, you can readily see the shift take place. You often will see a sigh of relief, a loosening of tension in the face, and a relaxing of the shoulders and posture in the chair. You also may feel your own body relax in sympathy.

Change. Once we have encountered a felt shift, we see our situation in a different perspective. Our *whole* situation seems different. We see

---

[28] Ibid., p. 86.

change as possible along lines of new meaning and direction. We feel empowered to change – to take new steps.[29]

By putting Focusing in a teachable form and making this inner process of change accessible, Gendlin has helped ease and restore the lives of many people. However, Gendlin has given us much more than Focusing. He also has given us a way to think about how we experience our life process, and how we conceptualize and express it. In a sense, Gendlin's work in psychotherapy has served him as a field laboratory for his philosophical work. Having some understanding of the felt sense makes Gendlin's philosophical work, particularly his conceptualization of how language works, easier to understand.

So, with this brief background on Focusing and the felt sense in hand, I want to turn to Gendlin's philosophical work to look more closely at the felt sense and our language use as a process.

---

[29] See E. Gendlin, 1964, "A Theory of Personality Change," in *Personality Change*, Phillip Worchel & Donn Byrne (Eds.), pp. 1-32 in on-line version at focusing.org.

3. Understanding Symbol Space

Gendlin's most recent and most comprehensive philosophical work is given in *A Process Model*.[1] This work, as the title suggests, conceptualizes our living as a process. It provides a model both for understanding how we are living and for thinking *further* about how we are living. Both the concepts and the conceptualizing are part of the same process. In this sense, we are "participants" in how we conceptualize our own living.

Some Basic Concepts

We spend most, if not all, of our lives living in what Gendlin calls "symbol space." Symbol space is the human environment that we have created. We form this space and are formed by it as we live our lives. Symbol space is complex. Despite this complexity, we can gain some initial understanding of symbol space, and more importantly how language works in this space, by looking at a few of Gendlin's basic concepts. I will lay these concepts out in a "bare bones" way by commenting on (and referencing) them. My comments are my own interpretation of Gendlin's concepts.[2] Since the concepts are experiential, you can test them, if you wish, by reflecting on your own experience and your own felt sensing of the concepts.

---

[1] E. Gendlin, 1997, *A Process Model*, abbreviated as APM. I also will reference E. Gendlin, 1997, *Experiencing and the Creation of Meaning*, abbreviated as ECM.

[2] Because his concepts are essentially open-ended, Gendlin asks that we clearly mark any interpretation as separate from his own. While I have tried to stay close to Gendlin's text, the interpretations are my own.

Experiencing

"Experiencing is concrete." It is what we feel inside when we say, I am feeling "this" way. We are self-aware of "this" feeling. We can turn our attention to it at any given moment. It is not fixed. It is not made up of discrete units. Our experiencing is more rich and intricate than we can conceptualize. It is always "more" than we can differentiate.[3]

Occurring into Implying

Experiencing is interacting. For example, we are constantly self-locating and self-registering our interacting with our physical environment. Consider that you have a feeling sense of what is behind you.

Try closing your eyes and sensing what is behind you.

Now that you have opened your eyes, try to recall your experience. Then, read on.

Each event (interacting) in a living process implies a further step. Each event is an occurring into an implying. In the example above, by turning your attention to your own sensing of what was behind you, your implying (some next step) likely was wanting to turn and visually verify what you were sensing. If you are in familiar surroundings, this wanting may only have been fleeting, and you may have just glanced up (after you opened your eyes) to confirm your surroundings. If you are in unfamiliar surroundings, you may have turned your head to verify what was behind you.[4]

In each interacting, we imply our next step. Our next step is implicit. It is *some* step, but it is not explicit. It only becomes explicit when we interact with our environment, with others, or with ourselves. Gendlin often uses hunger as a first teaching example of what he means by implying. Hunger implies feeding as a next step, but hunger is *not* hidden feeding. Normally, we would think of eating food as implied by

---

[3] E. Gendlin, ECM, pp. 27-29, and APM, p. 7-11.

[4] In this example, our feeling sense is the feeling of what we term "perception." Here it is a self-locating sense of where we are. It is a single sequence of both feeling and perception. E. Gendlin, APM, p. 96.

hunger. Say, however, that we eat some bad food, and throw up instead of digesting. Our hunger is paused, but still implied. In a real world case (assuming thoroughly bad food), some other feeding, like an IV feeding, could occur into hunger. Implying only implies *some* way forward, and occurring is *not* predetermined. When feeding occurs into hunger, the hunger is satisfied and changed into a new implying.[5]

The key point Gendlin makes with occurring into implying is that we (or any living process) imply our own change.

Life Carrying Forward

If our implying carries forward in an occurring (when we take an explicit step in an interaction), our implying changes into a *new* implying of some next step. We experience this change in implying as a feeling process. Occurring and implying are not separate events. All occurring occurs into an implying, but not all occurring carries implying forward. The primary distinction is between those events that carry life forward and those that do not.[6] We experience the sequence of occurring changes as a feeling process, as *continuity*.[7] We experience our own changing as carrying our living forward.

Eveing and Crossing

How do we imply our own change? Gendlin gives us two concepts to think further about implying: eveing and crossing. Eveing stands for *everything-by-everything*. Each implying forms freshly and includes all the ways some change *can* occur. Gendlin calls a freshly forming implying an eveing.[8] An eveing is all the changes that can occur, including the changes made to each other as they interaffect each other.

---

[5] E. Gendlin, APM, pp. 8-10.

[6] We have a bodily felt sense of the difference. When our interactions carry us forward, we experience a sense of "aliveness," and reflecting on our experience we may say something like, "I'm getting on with my life." When our interactions fail to carry us forward, we often experience a sense of "stuckness" and may say, "I'm stuck!" or something like, "I've hit a wall."

[7] E. Gendlin, APM, pp. 69-70.

[8] Ibid., pp. 38-46.

Crossing is a way of thinking about how these changes act on each other and on the whole.[9] We can say, for example, that crossing *opens* our past experiences, as aspects of all experiences that are *relevant* to the present occurring, and crosses them with each other, and with all possible ways that *can* happen as a way forward. In this sense, an eveving is an implicit crossing of everything-by-everything.[10] Moreover, we sense this implying (of everything-by-everything) as "coming to us" as a whole. Implying (eveving) and crossing take *no time*.

As an example, take your feeling sense of a close friend whom you like.[11] Say your friend's name is Julie, and you happen upon Julie on the street. You instantly "know" how tall Julie is, what she looks like, and what her mood is by her body looks and facial expression. You "know" all the ups and downs of your past relationship. Your feeling sense is not one of individual bits of information. Rather, your feeling sense comes as "all about Julie," and it comes "all at once." "All about Julie" also includes how you might talk to her, what tone of voice you may use, and what gestures you may use when you greet her. "All about Julie" shapes how you greet her. And you make your greeting *explicit*, "Hi, Julie…" Your speaking is the occurring (next step) into the implying of how you greet Julie.

Focaling

If an implying crosses everything-by-everything, why do we have one implying rather than many? In our "all about Julie" example (above) we greet Julie with a single greeting, "Hi, Julie…" We do not stop and "select" our greeting from a note card of greetings, "Hi, Julie…," Hello Julie…," "Hoya! Julie…," each with a different set of facial looks, body gestures and voice tones. In an implying, many

---

[9] Ibid., pp. 51-57. We will look at crossing in more detail when we discuss language use and metaphor on pp. 37-39 of these Notes.

[10] Ibid., pp. 42.

[11] Gendlin uses a similar example in E. Gendlin, 1981, pp. 33-34.

possible actions form into one possible action. Gendlin calls this aspect of implying, this many possible actions into one possible action – *focaling*.[12]

Let's look at a second example.[13] Say an artist is making a pencil drawing on paper. There are an infinite number of possible lines that the artist could draw. The artist pauses then draws a line. The artist does not try to draw all possible lines, nor does she "select" a line. The artist's implying crosses the already drawn lines (and her drawing skills) and she draws a line. We would say the artist *focals* the line. We ask the artist, "What happened?" The artist says, "The drawing *needed* something," adding, "and that was the *right* line."

How is that line the *right* line? The line is the right line because it makes a difference in the drawing (and the drawing process). We can say the line was *relevant* to the drawing.[14] The line carried the drawing forward. Many lines and their relationships may be relevant to crossing and forming the next line, but the next line is relevant only when it carries the drawing process forward. Drawing is not an arbitrary process. When the drawing process is carried forward, all that is involved in forming the next line was *relevant* to the previous lines. The artist not only draws the (from many into one) *one* next line, it is the *right* (relevant) line.[15]

If we took time now to speak with the artist, she might begin to describe her "aim" and the drawing's "direction." We commonly refer to our experience of events as having "purpose" or "direction." We experience our feeling sense of "aim" and "direction" as the crossing, focaling, and relevanting aspects of our implying. In this sense, we cross and focal many "purposes" and many possible "directions" into one action.

---

[12] E. Gendlin, APM, pp. 46-47. As you might guess, Gendlin makes up his own terms for some process aspects, like focaling, because there are no common words for the intended meaning.

[13] This example is taken from a similar example in E. Gendlin, APM, p. 47.

[14] Gendlin uses the word *relevanting* for this aspect of implying. Ibid., p. 47-49.

[15] Note. We can say the line is relevant only after it is drawn.

Gendlin makes the point that our sense of purpose and direction are part of our living process, from occurring into implying (carrying forward). Purpose and direction are aspects of our living process, they are not added on.

Symbol Space

Symbol space is the environment in which we interact. This environment is composed of interaction contexts, which we commonly call *situations*.[16] We engage symbolically in interactions. The power of a "symbolic act" lies in the fact that we do not have to be physically present (in space or time) to make changes in our life situation.[17]

As an example consider, if you will, that you have gone on the floor of the Chicago Mercantile Exchange (CME) and raised your fingers in a gesture that is understood by the commodity floor brokers. You likely will end up having to take possession of a railroad car full of pork bellies (or some other commodity) at a rail yard at some future (contract) date. You can go out on the street and make the same gesture, and nothing will happen (unless someone mistakenly thinks your gesture is obscene). We call your CME gesture an "action," and your street gesture a "doing."[18] The former gesture carries you forward in the situation, and the latter does not. It was (we would say) "inappropriate."

While we often use gestures, our situations largely are structured by language, by what we say in a given situation. Even our bodily processes are now structured by language. In order to pee at a friend's house, we first (commonly) say, "May I use your bathroom?" Our eating behavior also is highly structured: "Where would you like me to sit?" "Please pass the mashed potatoes!" And, "Yes, I would like some dessert."

---

[16] E. Gendlin, APM, p. 181. The concept of symbol space is laid out in APM, pp. 122-162, and pp. 163-215.

[17] Our symbol space has supplanted an earlier space, behavior space, an environment that we shared with other primates. Behavior space is "embedded" in symbol space. In behavior space, we likely needed to be physically present to interact and to carry forward an interaction context. See E. Gendlin, APM, pp. 102-103.

[18] Ibid., p. 167.

Our implying, even in these simple situations, includes our behavioral implying. In some situations, we directly display a behavioral response. Consider the following example: An experimenter places a young child in a learning experiment where the learning time to complete a task is purposely cut short. Informed that the time is up, the young child will lower his head, slightly canting it to one side, and look at the ground. We call this posture "embarrassment." You can elicit the same posture response in a young primate, an orangutan, in a similar learning situation that is cut short.[19] Later, we might guess that the young (human) child will learn to "cover up" his or her embarrassment in that *kind* of situation.

Our interactions in situations are not lost. What we call *language* and *culture* form in each interaction. Notice, we engage in only one interaction. Language and culture are not formed separately.[20] Culture is the collected interaction contexts in symbol space, and language is the collected use of words in interaction contexts. Our use of any word comes from "a family of uses."[21] In this sense, when we look in the dictionary we are looking at the *public* (collected) use of a word – what a word *means* comes from its use in different interaction contexts. The collected (public) uses of any one word usually far exceed what we, as individuals, have used. And, (as we look at a word's use-history in the dictionary) the change in these collected uses seems almost glacial.

We also collect word uses in experiencing our own interactions. What a word means to us *privately* usually exceeds its public meaning in any given situation since our own use includes all are our past uses of the word. Our use of any word has an internal/external aspect. Our "knowing" how to use a word in a situation comes to us as part our implying in the situation, our implying of the change we "need" in the situation. Words come to us as already crossed between their public use (use-family) and our situation.[22]

---

[19] I am indebted to Jeff Rulifson for this example.
[20] We can, if we wish, view them separately. See E. Gendlin, APM, pp. 196-199.
[21] The phrase is from Wittgenstein, quoted by Gendlin in APM, p. 52.
[22] Ibid., pp. 182-201. See also p. 289.

Some Implications

Looking at our living from a process point of view, I would like to focus on two key implications, which follow from Gendlin's basic concepts. These implications are how we think about time and expression.

Time[23]

We commonly think about time as linear time. We think of past, present, and future as positions on a timeline. Viewing our living as a process yields quite a different view of time. Our first impulse is to think of occurring as the present and implying as the future, but this is not the case. Occurring into implying gives a more intricate model of time. Occurring into implying carries our own implying forward so that we enact our own living, our own process. With this model, implying is changed if the process is carried forward, but implying always remains a part of the on-going occurring. The past and the future are the internal continuity of our body's own process. We experience time as an aspect of our on-going implying.[24]

When we think of our living in linear time we deny our own experiencing of implying and acting. Linear time is an observer's time. As observers, we view events as fixed units and put them into "time" segments.[25] However, when we "cut" events in this way, we drop out all internal connections between events. We are left with an artificial present with all the internal connections taken out. We have to add relationships back into our understanding of events. If there were no on-going implying, an occurring (event) would have no continuity, order, and connection to other events.

---

[23] I think it is essential to understand the concept of time in the process model in order to think further about forming a felt sense. The paragraphs on time that follow are mostly my condensing and editing Gendlin's APM text. I have done this to stay as close as possible to Gendlin on this point.

[24] Ibid., pp. 60-73.

[25] Note. An observer's time still requires an observer with continuity and memory to make comparisons between time points. Linear time, or any model of time, is not a prior condition for living.

With the process model, we see the aspect of our experiencing that we call "past," "present," and "future" depends on how it functions in occurring into implying. Occurring is a *type* of "present" and implying a *type* of "future." When we carry forward, our implying carries crossing, focaling, and relevanting as "future" forward functions. The "past" is what is gone on in. The "past" is a crossed past and functions in both the "present" and the "future" implying. This "past" is easier to understand if we remember that we are talking about an embodied process. Our "present" body is our regenerating "past." We are constantly "making" a new body.

Since we are so used to thinking in linear time, we can visualize what this "present" occurring into implying (carrying forward) looks like in linear time. As Gendlin suggests, a sequence of "present" events (occurring into implying) will look like a series of the Greek letter theta:[26]

ϑ   ϑ   ϑ   ϑ   ϑ   ϑ   ϑ

The linear "line" in each "present" (occurring) event appears to move forward into the "future," and then appears to move backward into the "past" to bring implying forward. Each "present" occurring changes *both* the "past" *and* the "future." The implying is internal to the process. Implying does not become the past. Implying changes as part of the on-going occurring. Implying implies its own change.

In the process model, there are no fixed time (or space) relationships.[27] Time relationships are regenerated in each (occurring) event. The "past" (antecedent) possibilities are not fixed. What is relevant is formed in each occurring. We only know the set of possibilities retroactively, after the event. This view contrasts with how we think with linear time where we assume a fixed set of possibilities. We think of the "present" as merely "filling out" a "past" possibility. When we think with a linear time model, we think what actually happens does not change the

---

[26] Ibid., pp. 72-73.

[27] Here we are talking about time relationships, but the implications are the same for (symbol) space relationships. Relationships in symbol space are regenerated in each occurring event.

predetermined set of possibilities. In this respect, with linear time we pretend to "know" what is relevant in advance.[28] The process model leads to past and future in the present. *The actual event changes the system of possibilities.* The possibilities, which the event regenerates, may not have been possibilities (in linear time) that entered into the event. In the process model, the now-present implying leads to a more intricate future, and the now-present past makes for a more complex past.[29]

Gendlin refers to our experiencing as time-inclusive.[30] By time-inclusive, Gendlin means that we can derive many models of time from our actual experiencing. The process model retains those time forward aspects of our living that we experience as human. In our implying, we "want" our life to work; we "want" to go on; and we "need" to succeed. Our carrying forward gives rise to purpose, direction, and meaning in our lives.

Expression

As you might guess from our brief look at time, a process model gives us a quite different understanding about how we might think about what we call expression.

Let's start with a common understanding of expression. We commonly think about expression as representing what we are feeling, or thinking, about a situation — as if we were broadcasting what we are feeling and thinking. Consider, however, that you are starting to express yourself, and the person with whom you are conversing rolls their eyes, showing no interest in what you are saying. Do you, or can you, keep talking? I know I can't keep talking. And, I would guess that you can't as

---

[28] We can still make predictions. Predictions are based on repeated observations. Both linear and process time models provide for predictions.

[29] The process time model bears similarities to current quantum physics where each event may be viewed as generating its own time-space relationships. How we choose to "explain" the event depends on the data we collect and the model we choose to use. Gendlin is aware of the similarities, see E. Gendlin, APM, p. 287.

[30] E. Gendlin, ECM, pp. 155-158.

well. If expression were purely a representation, then we should be able to keep talking.[31]

Expressing arises from the same basic process model. Expressing is interacting with our environment. We imply our participating environment.[32] In symbol space, this environment is the situation, the interaction context, and includes the other person. Expressing is occurring into implying. In expressing, you make your implying explicit by speaking to another in a situation. When you express yourself to another person, that person is *always already present* in your implying in the situation.[33] What each of us expresses in an interaction is already affected by the other. As you speak you imply *some* response, *some* feedback. When you receive a response that carries you forward, you continue by speaking further in the situation.

Gendlin calls expression a re-recognition.[34] We experience a series of bodily "feeling" changes of the situation as we carry forward in the situation. This series of "feeling" changes are our perceptions of our speaking *and* the other person's responses to our speaking. In process terms, when we express ourselves in a situation, we speak into our on-going implying of the situation. We re-recognize what we focally implied, and form a new implying. When we express ourselves we form a series of focal, relevant words or phrases. We are carried forward by our own speaking *and* by another's response to our words or phrases. In this sense, our expressing is both *reflexive* (bent back) as we hear ourselves speak, and *reflective* from another's response. By reflective I mean the other person reflects our speaking in some form. The other person's reflection affirms our sense of where we just "were." The first form of reflection (response) is empathy.[35]

---

[31] I could get angry and shout, but I would not be talking in the same way. I want to thank Rob Parker for this example.

[32] E. Gendlin, APM, p. 17.

[33] Ibid., p. 30.

[34] Ibid., pp. 238-239. For a discussion of recognition, see the section on recognition below.

[35] Ibid., p. 127.

Symbolizing Meaning

What we call meaning arises from interaction between our experiencing and symbols.[36] When we attend inwardly to some aspect of our feeling, or our feeling sense of a situation, we use symbols (words and gestures) to make *that* feeling explicit. To initially hold a feeling in our attention, we use words like "this," "that," or "it" as markers or pointers to *refer* to our feeling.[37] These markers have no meaning except to refer to our feeling. Once we symbolize (mark off) a feeling in this way, we can then further differentiate that feeling.

"What do you mean you are feeling like *that*?"

"I mean that I am feeling a bit scattered at this point."

"Why scattered?"

"I am bouncing around trying to tie together how we create meaning."

In the example above, I turned inward to my own feeling sense as I was writing about symbolizing. Gendlin makes the point that any aspect of our feeling can be symbolized and interpreted further. As he is fond of saying, "there is always more."[38] From a process point of view, we experience meaning by symbolizing (and conceptualizing) our implying. We make our implying explicit by speaking, thinking, or reading. Each explicit symbolizing act carries our on-going implying forward. There is always "more" to our implying than we symbolize and conceptualize. Viewing our symbolizing this way reverses how we commonly think about meaning. We commonly think that we create meaning when we speak and create order when we conceptualize. However, we experience meaning as a feeling or feeling sense. Our feeling sense of meaning is pre-conceptual. Our feeling sense arises in the body and is more "intricate" than any order that we symbolize.[39] We feel meaning as an

---

[36] E. Gendlin, ECM, p.1.
[37] Ibid., p. 100.
[38] Ibid., p. 16.
[39] Ibid., p. 24.

aspect of our on-going implying and we make *that* feeling explicit by speaking or thinking.

We are most intensely aware of experiencing meaning when symbols do not adequately symbolize our feeling or feeling sense of a situation. Gendlin makes this point of experiencing meaning by using the example of memory recall.[40] Consider the following example: A few days ago, I set down to work on these Notes having finished my breakfast and morning tea. I had the feeling sense that I had forgotten something. I "knew" that I had forgotten something that I wanted "to do," or more precisely I had a "knowing" that I was missing a "to do." This feeling of "knowing" was both vague and precise. As I sat with this feeling I tried out a few of my usual "to do's." Nothing fit. Finally, "Clip the article on monkeys" popped into my head, and I gave a sigh of relief. I had wanted to clip an article on primate behavior from my morning newspaper. My felt sense of meaning was "there" as a referent for my seeking. I experienced a further sense of "meaning" when the explicit "clip the article" fit my sense of the missing "want to do."[41] This was, as we would say, a "meaningful" experience for me.

Recognition

Besides having a symbol refer directly to a feeling or a feeling sense, we use symbols to "call forth" a felt sense of meaning for us. We call this act of "calling forth" — recognition.[42] When we use symbols (words, gestures, images, or things) in this way, we form a feeling sense of meaning (a felt meaning) from the symbols. Symbols used in this way have a public meaning, which is independent of our private meaning use. Reading is a form of recognition. When we read, the sequence of word symbols "calls forth" a present felt meaning for us by opening and crossing (everything by everything) our own past experiences with the public meaning (and crossing) of each word in the sequence. Notice your own experience as you read this sequence. What is going into forming

---

[40] Ibid., p. 92.

[41] For other modes of felt meaning in cognition, see ECM, pp. 90-137. Problem solving has a similar "Ah Ha!" feeling aspect. See ECM, p. 71.

[42] Ibid., pp. 105-106.

your own felt meaning of what *recognition* means to you now? I am guessing your reasons for reading this piece, other authors and other philosophical works. I would guess that there is likely some carry over from our preceding discussions of occurring into implying, crossing, and focaling. I also would guess some sense of whether you like, or dislike this style of writing. And what else? I am sure there is "more." Once a felt sense of meaning has formed, you can always find "more" there.

Explication

What we do with the "more," we call explication. When we explicate, we further differentiate our feeling sense of meaning "of" or "about" a topic or situation. Each word or word sequence that we put together is an occurring into our implying in the situation. We carry ourselves forward with each explicit sequence into our "seeking" to understand (and provide an understanding of) the situation or topic at hand. From the many meaning possibilities in our on-going implying, we create an explicit sequence. Let's take as an example, the word "fairness." "Fairness" comes to mind because of the article (mentioned above) that I clipped about monkeys displaying a sense of fairness in sharing food.[43] When I refer to my own sense of the meaning of "fairness," it includes the notions of equitable and reasonable as in "fair play" or a "fair trial." I have held the quite reasonable idea that this was exclusively a human trait. However, my sense of the meaning now extends to include the possibility that "fairness" is an aspect of primate behavior that arises from the need to "share and cooperate" in an activity like eating. So, my own sense of the meaning of "fairness" now is that it is embedded more deeply (as a behavioral aspect) in our own human living process. Let me put this sense of "fairness" into a few sentences:

"Fairness means an equitable process or outcome. Fairness comes from our need to share and cooperate with one another. Fairness is embedded in cooperative behaviors that we likely share with other primates."

---

[43] Sharon Begley, "Animals Seem to Have an Inherent Sense of Fairness and Justice," *Wall Street Journal*, November 10, 2006, p. B1.

There is "more" if I chose to go on, but I will stop this explication by "sticking a pin it."[44]

Making the explication, I experienced a more differentiated meaning of the word "fairness." I acquired a deeper sense of the relational aspects of the meaning, and I have a full sense that I have symbolized only part of my presently held meaning of "fairness." Each word sequence from "fair play" and "fair trial" to "primate behavior" to "sharing and cooperation" was an opening and crossing of many meaning possibilities. The presently held meaning that I "have" exceeds the sentences that I put down. Again, from a process standpoint an implying always carries a more intricate order than what occurs (what we say or write). Since what we say or write carries our implying forward, our saying or writing always carries more meaning possibilities than we actually make.[45] We experience this aspect of our saying and writing as "unfinished." If we focus on our sense of a meaning, there is always more at the "edge."

At first glance it appears that this aspect of opening and crossing at word junctures enables us to shift from one meaning context to another in a short period of time. By extension, it would appear that we could turn our attention to any topic or situation at any time. We cannot. We cannot turn our attention to something that is not connected to what we are living, feeling, or thinking. In symbol space, the subject or situation must "come to us." It must connect in some way to our present situation.[46]

Try an Experiment

Let's try an experiment with a felt sense of meaning. In his writing, Gendlin often uses a symbol of a sequence of three dots ... to indicate a slot for a felt sense in a sentence.[47]

---

[44] "Stick a pin it" is one of my favorite expressions and I have been waiting for a place to stick it in the text. So, I stuck it here.

[45] E. Gendlin, APM, p. 69, and p. 154.

[46] Ibid., p. 201.

[47] I drew this exercise from a teaching story in E. Gendlin, 1991, "Thinking Beyond Patterns," in *The Presence of Feeling in Thought*, p.18 in the on-line version at focusing.org.

I will set out a sentence with a slot ... in it; followed by a phrase with a second slot ... Please complete the sentence while giving some attention to your own experience as you do so. Take your time to let your feeling sense of the first slot ... form. Then, let the follow-on phrase ... form. Give yourself some more time to see if you want to make any additional word changes to the sentence. When you are satisfied with your wording, write out your sentence in the line space below.

Here is the sentence:

Walking alone in the park at dusk, I felt ..., so I ... .

....

Consider the following questions about your experience, and we will compare notes.

Have you written this exact sentence before? I'm guessing likely not. What word or words came to you to fill in the first slot ...? What was your experience like in forming the word or words?

When you filled in the first slot ..., how did the follow-on phrase come? Did it feel the same, or did it feel different?

After you filled in the follow-on phrase, were you drawn to go back and change the wording in the first part of the sentence, or in any part of the sentence?

Please return to your felt meaning of the sentence. Is there more meaning in the sentence that you have yet to express?

Let me fill in my own responses (as I am writing these lines), so we can compare notes.

As soon as I set out the sentence with the first slot ..., I had a feeling sense of sadness. I felt "sad":

Walking alone in the park at dusk, I felt *sad*,

The follow-on phrase came to me as: so I "turned and went home."

Walking alone in the park at dusk, I felt *sad*, so *I turned and went home*.

After completing the sentence, I wanted to change the wording to:

Walking alone in the park at dusk, I felt sad *because my friends were not there*, so I turned and went home.

This sentence led me to two more changes. Here is my sentence with the last changes:

Walking alone in *Jackson Square* at dusk, I felt sad because my friends were not there, so I turned and *walked* home.

Here are my comments on my sentence forming:

As I indicated, the feeling sense of "sad" came to me swiftly as I wrote out the sentence. There may have been other words, but they fell away quickly. The "sad" also had a feeling of *opening up*, as if my experiences were opening. This opening up was filled quickly by my sense of a small park, Jackson Square, in the French Quarter in New Orleans. My experience with this first (felt meaning) ... was that it was a *focaling*, forming many meanings into one meaning. It "knew" what could be said. In this sense, the (felt meaning) ... was both open *and* precise.[48]

The follow-on phrase, the second (felt meaning) ..., "so I turned and went home" came swiftly as well. My feeling sense was that this phrase came out of the sadness. The first felt meaning, once expressed, led directly to forming the follow-on phrase. It had a role in saying what could be said *further*.

When I set down the phrase "so I turned and went to go home," I wanted to expand (explicate) the sentence to include "because my friends were not there." When I walked to Jackson Square in the evening, I often met friends to go to a bar for drinks and talks about writing. When

---

[48] Added Note. My response in this exercise is an example showing that the crossing aspects of a past experiencing only form relevantly in the actual occurring (here the writing of a sentence). Prior to completing the sentence, I would never have guessed that I would draw upon my experiences in New Orleans some forty years ago.

the follow-on words came, they forced a revision in the already written words. In my own experience (and in Gendlin's terms), the written words implied *something* that would revise those words. *The words implied their own revision, their own change.*

The revised wording implied a *further* revision that led to my wanting to make the sentence more specific. I changed the "park" to "Jackson Square," and changed "went" to "walked." I always walked to and from the square.

When I returned to my completed sentence, the felt meaning for me was a sense of present sadness and loss – for these friends are lost to me (I have lost track of them) and I am unlikely to see them again.

The ... is an implying. Normally, we do not notice this implying when we are speaking or writing – unless we lack the phrases for *what* is implied, as was the intended case here for me in this experiment, and (hopefully) for you as well.

How Words Work

Our experiment in forming a sentence (above) shows that when words form they imply their own revision, their own change. Words form from our bodily sense of living in a situation. Words work by reconstituting how we (collectively) carry life forward in a situation. In this sense, each word is its own occurring into an implying. Each word is its own carrying forward of its own implicit sequences within a situation. Each word crosses with previous words and forms *some* possible next word or phrase. When we speak in a situation we *use* this aspect of words, their own implying and carrying forward, to carry us forward in a situation. In Gendlin's terms, we carry ourselves forward *mediately* (by means of) using words in a situation.[49]

Consider a common situation as an example. Let's say that you are hurrying to work, walking across the lobby of your office building. You inadvertently bump into someone coming the other way. You look up and say, "I'm sorry." The words just come out without any attention on

---

[49] E. Gendlin, APM, pp. 188-189.

your part. In most cases, the other person takes your words as an apology. He may say something like, "That's OK," and you both move on. You have used "I'm sorry" to mediately carry you through the bumping situation. However, say that the person does not respond in an amicable way, rather he steps sideways partially blocking your way. The person (and the situation) then demands your attention. You look up and say, "I'm terribly sorry. I'm late for work and I'm rushing." You get a slight nod in response, and continue, "I overslept. I didn't want to be late. I've got a project to finish. I'm sorry. I should have looked where I was going!" Those words are enough, and he steps aside.

In this second more differentiated case, you are using words and crossing them by attending to your feeling sense of the situation. The words you use are opening and crossing, reconstituting a sequence (a pattern) that will carry you forward in the situation. In this sense, your use of words is a re-crossing of the words and their implied sequences and your own experience of words that you have used in similar situations.[50] You are re-crossing two contexts, the words' own contexts, and the interaction context (the bumping situation) that you are in now. Notice that while the implied words and implied sequences in this simple situation are quite large, only certain words form in the situation, and only in relation to other words, and only in certain places in the sequence.[51] You likely would not elicit an amicable response by saying, "I'm late for work and I'm rushing" without saying "I'm sorry." Our sense of the situation usually leads us to say, "I'm sorry" and then to differentiate (explain) why we bumped the other person.

Metaphor

If we look more closely at our bumping situation, we can see that our common use of language is metaphorical. How is it that we "know" our

---

[50] Ibid., p. 194.

[51] What we call syntax, the structure of our language use, arises from this implicit aspect of words. Each word implies what comes next both in terms of the interaction context and the sequence of words that may follow. Syntax is far more complex (and difficult to reduce to simple rules) than we might expect from looking at just sequence order alone. For more comments on syntax, see E. Gendlin, APM, pp. 190-191.

bumping situation is an "I'm sorry" situation? Our "knowing" has two aspects. First, our "knowing" is pre-conceptual and arises from our feeling sense of the situation. Second, when we cross possibilities (of words or word sequences) in our implying in the situation, we "know" that this situation is *like* other situations we have experienced. If I ask myself how I "know" this situation is an "I'm sorry" situation, I reply (to myself) that it is that *kind* of situation. It is *like* when I spill food on someone at the dining table, or when I step over someone's feet while making my way down a theater aisle. Our use-family of words is (collectively) a collection of kinds of interaction contexts. And our own collecting of (word) uses also is a collecting of kinds of interactions.

These metaphorical aspects of crossing give us the ability to readily speak in new situations, and to readily create new meanings. In any new situation, what we call a "use-family" of a word is our feeling sense of the many situations in which we have used the word.[52] This "use-family" crosses freshly with the new situation where we are faced with speaking. In crossing the "use-family" opens and crosses with our sense of the new situation and we can speak. Our speaking will be more than we might expect from just our previous word use alone. The opening and crossing can create a new use and a new meaning. If the opening and crossing do not take place, then we are not able to speak. We will be at a "loss for words."

If these comments on metaphor begin to have an odd ring to them, it is because looking at metaphor from a process point of view reverses the order of the way we usually think about metaphor.[53] We usually think about metaphor as combining existing similarities from two words or phrases From a process point of view, our felt sense of meaning arises from the implicit crossing of the words or phrases. Then, when we have a sense of the meaning, we "work out" the similarities that arise from our new sense of meaning. The occurring (thinking, speaking or writing the metaphor) shapes the meaning.

---

[52] Here I am using "use-family" to indicate our own collection of uses.
[53] Gendlin puts forward his concept of metaphor in APM, pp 51-54, and in ECM, pp. 113-117.

We can get a better "feel" for the metaphor process by playing with a few metaphors. I will suggest two metaphors, relate my experiences, and ask you to sense your own experience. Let's create a metaphor, "My love is like the sun." I haven't made this metaphor before. When I spoke (and wrote) the words, I had an immediate sense that they crossed, and that I could work out some meaning. I can work out, "My love shines bright in my life. She gives me warmth and sustains me." The working out comes easily. I also have the sense that, if I chose, I could take more meaning from the metaphor. Now, consider crossing "The sun is like my love." Here I get a sense of some meaning. The meaning is more elusive. I can work out that "The sun is a constant in my life. It is always there for me." Again, I sense that more meaning is there, but I really will have to work at it. Notice, if you will, that the crossing is not symmetrical.[54] When we form metaphors, the crossing direction makes a difference. Finally, try crossing "A worm is like the sun." I can't get this one to cross. When I try, I get a "poof" inside. For me, there is nothing there. If I try to force a meaning, I get a "thunk" in my head.

When we form (and use) metaphors, the crossing process is, as Gendlin would say, quite precise. It is not an arbitrary process. Metaphors form (words cross) in a bodily way because they can open and cross to form a new meaning. Gendlin calls this aspect of our speaking (and living): the "Law of Occurrence."[55] What occurs, occurs because it *can* occur. We only "know" the why and the how *after* the occurring. We create new meanings in our implying (opening and crossing) in a situation. We only develop our concepts to "explain" our language use after the fact.[56]

---

[54] When we open and cross past experiences with a present situation, we usually do so metaphorically by conceptualizing in the direction the "present" is like the "past."

[55] E. Gendlin, APM, p. 52.

[56] This is conceptually the same form (schematic) as regenerating the system of time-space possibilities in an event. Here we regenerate (shape) the meaning possibilities (similarities) arising in a metaphor by speaking (the event).

Before Moving On

Before moving on, I would like to pause and return to my intent in laying out Gendlin's conceptualizing of our living process. In order to understand how we might get beyond words, I wanted to provide (and hopefully have provided) some understanding of *what* it means to say we have a felt sense of a situation in this complex environment that we call symbol space. And I wanted to provide an understanding of *how* we now use language (words) to carry our lives forward in situations. Our present language use structures how we live, and we refer to our felt sense to shape our speaking and acting – our own changing in our life situations.

When we think about our living from a process point of view, we clearly "know" less than we commonly assume about our experiences in living. To borrow a phrase from George Fox, we have become bound by our own "notions" of what is possible or not possible in our living. Our common notions of time and expression are self-limiting. From a process standpoint, we shape all possibilities (everything-by-everything) in any present situation. We only can know the "why" and "how" after we move "to meet" a situation. To think that we "know" the possibilities of our living beforehand is, I think, a too simplistic view of our own experiencing.

4. Living in Symbol Space

Having sketched out how Gendlin constructs language working in symbol space, I want to take some time to comment on aspects of *living* in that space. I am going to draw on my own experiences and reference comments from Gendlin. I will try to make a clear separation between my own reflections and Gendlin's comments. I want to share these experiences because I think the complexity in our living now makes it more difficult for us to change our life situations *and*, at the same time, drives us to seek changes.

> *Let us go then, you and I,*
> *When the evening is spread out against the sky…*
> *Let us go and make our visit.*[1]

Slotted Feelings

What we consider culture is the routine patterned situations where we interact with others. Just as we "know" implicitly what we may say in a given situation, we also "know" or "expect" what we may feel in a given situation. Let me take a simple example of gift giving. I have an in-law who has a penchant to select gifts (for me), which I neither like, nor can use. When we are gathered for holiday gift giving, I "know" that I should feel gratitude and joy when I receive and open my gift. Besides saying "Thank you," I smile and feel "thankful." In saying "Thank you" and feeling (partly) "thankful," I carry the situation forward and the gift giving moves on around the family circle.

---

[1] These and the following italicized lines are from T.S. Eliot, 1917, "The Love Song of J. Alfred Prufrock," in *Prufrock and Other Observations*, on-line at Bartleby.com.

Now, I am not faking my "thankful" feeling. I am thankful that I have been accepted in the family circle, and that I am included in the gift giving. I focus on *that* feeling, setting aside the small discomfort of knowing that I will recycle the gift via Goodwill at some later date. What I am relating here is what Gendlin calls "slotted feelings."[2] While we often consider our internal feeling life private, what we often experience is a series of feelings in routine "slots" where we expect the feelings (and words) to carry the situation forward. These slotted feelings are public. In this case, these implicit feelings are known both to me and to my in-law. The expected feelings are implicit for both of us in our "sense" of the situation. If I were to grimace and show discomfort at my gift, then the situation likely would come to a halt. I would then face a markedly changed situation. I choose not to take that path because I want to "get on" with the evening.

As I reflect on my moving from situation to situation, feeling into these patterned "slots," I have a sense of "jaggedness" and a wearying unease in my "feeling life." I certainly do not feel fully alive in situations of the *kind* I have described. I feel disconnected inside when I set aside my feelings, or some of my feelings, in a situation like *that*. Still, I choose to carry the situation forward, if only partly, rather than to invest time and energy, not to say the discomfort of "going into" my feelings more deeply. This is what we mean, I think, when we say, "I am sliding by."

> *And indeed there will be time...*
>
> *Time for you and time for me,*
> *And time yet for a hundred indecisions,*
> *And for a hundred visions and revisions,*
> *Before the taking of toast and tea.*
>
> *In the room the women come and go*
> *Talking of Michelangelo.*

---

[2] When we learn what to "say" in a situation, we also learn what to "feel" in a situation. Often we are taught a "should feel" directly, or indirectly along with a "should say." As in the example here, I learned that I should always feel "thankful" for a gift. See E. Gendlin, APM, p. 217.

Role Complexity[3]

I have started speaking about *living* in routine patterns with a simple instance of gift giving. Consider now, if you will, the larger culturally patterned routines – the roles that we are called upon to play in life, son, daughter, husband, wife, father, and mother. Clearly these routines are more complex than in previous times. I am thinking now of my own father and mother. My father died three years ago. My mother died earlier this year. They both were in their nineties when they died, and had been married almost seventy years when my father died.

Having sorted through their personal papers, I am struck by how simple their lives were compared to my own life. A thin manila folder holds all their personal papers, single sheets of birth and death certificates, one marriage license, and a simple living trust. I never had an explicit conversation with my father about what to expect in the role of husband and father. However, I can readily imagine sitting in his basement workshop and listening to what he might say:

"Son, your mother asked me to talk to you about being a husband and father."

"What do you mean?"

"She wants you to know what to expect, what is expected of you."

"OK."

"The first thing about being a husband is that you put bread on the table. No matter what, no matter how hard it is – you put bread on the table. Next, you take care of looking after the cars and the heavy stuff around the house. It's your wife's job to cook, clean up, and look after the kids… If your wife wants you to go to church, go to church if it makes her happy. Save some time for yourself, save some time to go out with your friends – play golf, have a beer, and play some cards… If things get testy with your wife, back off… The main thing is to put up with each other."

"Don't you love mom?"

---

[3] For Gendlin's comments on role complexity, see APM, p. 227.

"Of course, I do. Don't get me wrong. But, in marriage the main thing is to be willing to put up with each other. That's the main thing."

"OK."

"For kids, you teach them right from wrong. Smack them if you have to, but make sure they know right from wrong. Teach them what you know. Just like I taught you how to use each and every tool in this workshop. If you have boys, play with them. Take them fishing. Show them how to field ground balls."

"Is that all?"

"Yes, that's about it ... Oh, be kind and help others when you can."

I got to know my father quite well in the end. He had Alzheimer's the last fifteen years of his life. I was the primary care giver for him (and for my mother). I cared for them through the progressive end stages of their lives, from independent living, through assisted living, and into hospice care for my father. The last few weeks of his life, when others would come into the room he would look at them, smile and say, "This is my son. He's a good son. He's looking after me!" He was quite certain about the role of a "good son." I chose to live into that role. He died holding my hand.

Now, I am looking over at the shelf holding my personal papers. I count three two-inch binders and a one-inch binder. These papers represent four marriages, three divorces, and two moderately complex trusts providing for my wife Becky and my three sons. I raised my eldest son Alex as a single parent from infancy until he was seven. Then, I married again, had two more sons, divorced again, and raised Alex as a single parent through his teen years. I was the absent parent for my two younger sons, Dylan and Brandon. Absent in the sense that after our divorce they lived on the east coast with their mother. I saw them on holidays and for short summer visits when they stayed with me. Over time, as I talked regularly on the phone with them (and still do), I fell into the role of being a "sensitive" parent, one likely to talk about feelings, needs, and relationships.

Nothing in my upbringing prepared me for these situations. My life roles as husband and father turned out to be far more complex than my father's. What do you do when you are a single parent with a young boy? How do you put together childcare? Is it better to work part-time until he is in school? What do you do if he has a nosebleed in the middle of the night and you can't stop it? Nothing in my father's routines came close to helping me handle my own life situations – least of all "putting up with someone." I didn't, and the first three women I married certainly did not "put up" with me. Nothing came easily for me. I had to pick and choose how I would handle my husband, not-husband, and father-mother roles. More often than not, I got "stuck," or at my best just "muddled through."

> *And indeed there will be time*
> *To wonder, "Do I dare?" and, "Do I dare?"*
>
> *... ... ...*
>
> *Do I dare*
> *Disturb the universe?*
> *In a minute there is time*
> *For decisions and revisions which a minute will reverse.*
>
> *For I have known them all already, known them all: –*
> *Have known the evenings, mornings and afternoons,*
> *I have measured out my life with coffee spoons…*

Structure-Bound

How did I get stuck? Mostly I got stuck in forms of my own devising. As I look back, I always considered myself an "outsider."[+] Early on, I formed an idea of independence. I always viewed myself as an outsider, as "not fitting in" with groups. In my working roles, I sought independence by choosing to work for myself with several early failures and some later success. I set difficult goals and sought to meet them by working incredibly long hours. I was a "workaholic." Besides the normal attrition that such behavior takes on family life, I paid an internal price. I could never open up

---

[+] I was greatly influenced by Colin Wilson's book *The Outsider* characterizing the intellectual as a social outsider. The current edition is from Penguin Putnam, 1982.

and reveal to my then wife or young children my own fears and feelings – my fears of failure, insecurity, and responsibility. I shut down. Having to devise my own way of working and being a father, I could not find a way that fully worked for me. For long stretches of time I was bound by an "outsider" structure of my own creation, dragging myself through each day. I did not find a way that brought me joy and freshness.[5]

I think my own experiences of role complexity are quite common. I could not in any way make my father's roles work for me. I could see that my own life was far more complex, and got even more complex as I went along. In picking and choosing how to maneuver through my situations as husband and father, I tried to devise solutions as best I could. Only now, with the help of my wife Becky have I got on to the way of "opening up" and sharing my feelings, fears, and needs. Certainly, I feel more "sensitive" now in my own way of being with others.

> *Should I, after tea and cakes and ices,*
> *Have the strength to force the moment to crisis?*
> *But though I have wept and fasted, wept and prayed,*
>
> ... ...
>
> *I am no prophet – and here's no great matter;*
> *I have seen the moment of my greatness flicker,*
> *And I have seen the eternal Footman hold my coat and snicker,*
> *And in short I was afraid.*

Thinned Living

When I re-read the following passage from Gendlin in order to reference it, I had a small laugh because in the past few weeks I have engaged in several "symbolic actions" as he describes them.

> Even aside from the fact that our routines don't work anymore, the complexity of urban educated literate living

---

[5] For Gendlin's comments on being structure-bound, see E. Gendlin, 1964, Op. cit. p.16. See also "hard-structures" in APM, p. 258.

consists so largely of symbolic actions rather than bodily doings, that they are 'thinned'... Of course, when signing something or pushing a button, such a vast change is made, we normally feel that quite distinctly in the body. The stomach sinks, the heart pounds, the hand shakes, or, if the action is fully carrying forward, there is a flood of relief and a new dawn on life. But how often are our actions that change making? Usually the whole remains, only slightly altered.[6]

In the past few weeks I have switched to a new computer (a Mac), ending a twenty-year love-hate relationship with Microsoft. I also brought in a DSL line and attached a wireless network for my Mac (and Becky's new Mac). I engaged in the "symbolic act" of signing my name on a line on paper at the local Mac store, and again at my internet service provider's office. I never before noticed this hand gesture – of signing my name. This simple gesture in these two different contexts provided for changes in my life. Please notice that this physical act is the same. Of course, the social context is understood. In fact, I normally don't think about it, and I am sure that you do not as well. When I was in the Mac store, it crossed my mind (fleetingly) to sign the paper, and then ask for a more expensive model. I can imagine the perplexed response that I might have got, "No, that is not what we meant. That is not what we meant at all. You signed for the other one."

Bringing up the new machine and a network was a trial for me. These are not things I like to do. After a struggle with the DSL line (one piece of equipment was labeled backwards), my finger shook and my heart pounded as I hit the Mac key turning on the DSL line. What a relief, the line worked. Of course, that moment is faded now. I take my new machine and new internet access speed for granted. My life is only slightly altered at best.

---

[6] E. Gendlin, APM, p. 228.

And would it have been worth it, after all,
After the cups, the marmalade, the tea,
Among the porcelain, among some talk of you and me,

… … …

It is impossible to say just what I mean!

… … …

If one, settling a pillow or throwing off a shawl,
And turning towards the window, should say:

'That is not it at all,
That is not what I meant, at all.'

Always Within Our Situation

Putting aside the usual statistics on family breakups, divorce, and perpetual churn in jobs and careers, my own life experience shows me that our traditional roles, our culturally patterned routines no longer work. We are left to our own devices. What we devise works only partly to carry our life situation forward. In a certain sense, the routines we devise have become too complex to carry forward in symbol space. Our emotional life is "thinned." We certainly can open up and make our own internal feeling-life and thinking known. We can more finely differentiate our interactions. We can, and do, seek others who are trying to "open up" and reveal themselves. However, even when we do reveal more of our inner life, we still encounter what I call a background fear – a nagging fear that we can never "get things right" in our life situation, or that we can never *really* change our life situation.

I grow old… I grow old…
I shall wear the bottoms of my trousers rolled.

Shall I part my hair behind? Do I dare eat a peach?
I shall wear white flannel trousers, and walk upon the beach.

I have heard the mermaids singing, each to each.
I do not think they will sing to me.

A Modern Quaker Query

Quakers are fond of what we call "queries." These are questions about life that we ask ourselves. More often than not, no ready answer comes. Mostly, we sit with the question and see what comes. Before moving on to the next section on change and transformation, ask yourself,

"What would I do if I were not afraid?"[7]

---

[7] Martha Manglesdorf, 1994, quoted by C. Whitmire, 2001, *Plain Living*, on p. 73.

5. Change and Transformation

Hopefully having gained some understanding of how we use language and live in symbol space, let's return now to our original question of how language works as we seek change and transformation:

"How is it possible to use words to learn to get beyond words in order to speak (use) words in a new way?"

Three Language Sequences

I want first to look at this question by examining language sequences from Quaker, Focusing, and NVC practices. These practices, in my own experience, lead to change and transformation. In each practice, these sequences are the basis for our "using words to learn to get beyond words." By basis, I mean that these sequences are the means by which people learn and teach each practice.

The three sequences are set out in the Table of Language Sequences below.[1]

Turning Inward and Questioning

When we look at these sequences, we can see that each sequence calls for an inward looking and a questioning. In Quaker Meditation, this initial questioning often takes the form of asking, "What is really going on in my life?" or, "What is really going on in my Meeting?" In Focusing, an initial questioning often is "What wants my awareness?" At first glance, it might seem that NVC has a different form. I have set out NVC in its

---

[1] The Quaker sequence is my own adaptation from R. Ambler, 2002, *Light to live by*; the Focusing sequence is from E. Gendlin, 1981, *Focusing*; and the NVC sequence is from M. Rosenberg, 2003, *Nonviolent Communication*.

Table – Language Sequences Leading to Change and Transformation

Quakers	*Focusing*	*NVC*
Mind the Light Relax body and mind…	**Clearing a Space** What wants my awareness?	**Observations** When I see (hear, remember, imagine)… When you see (hear, remember, imagine)…
Question What is going on in my life? Or, what is going on in my Meeting?	**Felt Sense** Sense what comes…	**Feelings** I feel… Do you feel…?
Open Your Heart Focus on one concern…	**Get a Handle** What is the feeling quality of the felt sense?	
Wait in the Light Why is it like that?	**Resonate** Go back and forth between the quality word and the felt sense. Is that right?	**Needs** Because I need… Because you need…?
Truth Welcome the truth…	**Ask** What does it need? Or, what does it want me to know?	
Reflect Consider how you need to act…	**Receive** Welcome what comes…	**Requests** Would you be willing to…? Would you like me to…?

dialogue form where the speaker's role is given as statements: "I am feeling…" and "Because I need…" In practice, when NVC is used for self-empathy, or as an internal dialogue in the course of a conversation, these are asked as questions: "What am I feeling?" and "What am I needing?" in this situation.

Following this initial questioning, all three sequences (and practices) look for a response. For Quakers, the response looked for is called the "truth." In Focusing, it is the forming of the "felt sense." For NVC, the response looked for is a "need." I plan to look at each of these sequences and practices in more detail. For now, I simply want to call your attention to the common language pattern calling for an inward turning, a questioning, and an expecting of a response.

Interacting

Clearly we have an interacting here: a questioning and an expecting of a response. If we turn our attention in this way, how is *this* questioning different than any other questioning we might make of ourselves? With *what* are we interacting?

Let me lay out an answer:

When we question in this way, we are interacting with our own implying.

I will describe the process that led me to this answer, and follow on with some implications I see that arise from this answer.

Light Meditation

Since many of you may not be familiar with Quaker practices, I want to start by describing the Quaker Meditation, which we call "Light Meditation." Light Meditation, as we practice it, is the modern form of an early Quaker practice. Rex Ambler, a contemporary English Quaker scholar, reconstructed the Meditation from the early letters and writings of George Fox. Ambler called his reconstructed form "Experiment with Light," and described the practice in a small book, *Light to live by*. [2]

---

[2] R. Ambler, 2002, *Light to live by*.

Ambler's reconstruction led to a four-step Meditation:[3]

> Mind the light.
>
> Open your heart to the truth.
>
> Wait in the light.
>
> Submit to the truth.

This Meditation makes use of the Quaker concepts of the inward light and truth, and the Quaker practice of "waiting." The inward light is the "pure light of God." It "is that which makes you aware."[4] From an experiential standpoint, the inward light is an inner awareness or an inner knowing. To "mind the light" is to turn to this inner awareness. As we set out in the Introduction to these Notes, truth is the reality of our life. It is our life as "it really is" – without the stories that we tell ourselves and tell others about ourselves. Turning to an inner awareness shows us, "discloses" in Fox's words, those stories and imaginings that we tell ourselves.[5] It is just those stories, imaginings, and "notions" that keep us from fully living. When we "wait in the light" or "stand still in the light," we can see our life situation as it really is, stripped of all pretenses. The "truth" comes from "waiting in the light." If we "submit to the truth," or in a more modern phrase "welcome the truth," then we are empowered to change our life situation – to live our lives in a new way.

In the course of practicing and testing this four-step Light Meditation, Rex Ambler came across Gendlin's *Focusing* book. He immediately saw similarities between Light Meditation and Focusing. When Ambler practiced Focusing, he found that Focusing provided a more practical lead in to Meditation. Focusing helped "center" awareness in the body. Centering in this way gets us more easily (and more reliably) past our "modern thinking mind," where we spend most

---

[3] Ibid., pp. 16-22.

[4] Ibid., p. 16.

[5] Ibid., p. 20.

of our waking moments.[6] Focusing also provided a form of questioning, which further helped to focus attention in Meditation.

Ambler incorporated these elements of Focusing in putting together a modern six-step form of the Light Meditation.[7] Quakers learn and practice this Meditation as a guided meditation, meeting in small groups called "Light groups." Following Meditation, the group sets aside a time for journaling experiences from the Meditation. After journaling, the group shares experiences in a round of sharing – each person sharing as much or as little as he or she feels comfortable in sharing. Quakers practice the Meditation as a community experience. While the content of the Meditation may be, and often is quite personal, the support and trust for change comes from the listening and caring of the other participants. Once learned, a person also may take on the Meditation as a personal practice. In my own case, I have adopted the Meditation as a personal practice.

I have set out my own adaptation of Ambler's six steps in Appendix A to these Notes.[8] These steps along with a few key phrases are:

1. Relax. Settle into silence. Let yourself become aware.

2. What is really going on in your life? Let your real concerns emerge.

3. Focus on one concern. Let the light show you the concern.

4. What does it want you to know? Let the truth reveal itself.

5. When the answer comes, welcome it.

6. Consider how you need to act.

From a Quaker point of view, we have a Meditation of "waiting in the light" with an overlay of Focusing guidance. From a Focusing point of view, we have a familiar sequence done in a group setting with new symbols ("light" and "truth"), and the addition of a last step asking for

---

[6] Ibid., p. 32.

[7] Ibid., pp. 37-38, and Appendix, pp. 45-53.

[8] In Appendix A.

action, for a next step in the situation. Some Focusers include this last step in their Focusing, but many do not.

I want to set out a series of Light Meditations, which I journaled over four months. These Meditations form the basis for my writing these Notes. After setting out these Meditations, I will resume our discussion.

Meditations

After settling in, I asked what is really going on [for me] in Meeting?[9] And what is my role with Quakers? I felt a familiar pain around the inside of my heart. I sat with the pain, looking for other feelings. Nothing came, so I returned to the pain around my heart. It felt both long-standing and freshly insistent. It held a quality of aching and longing. After sitting with this sense [for a time] an image formed – like a wooden bow of a ship poking up through the ground. After some more time, I sensed people around the poked-up bow. The ground around [the bow] was grassy and green. When I sought the truth, and the next step forward for me, the word "mapping" came to me along with an image of a brown map spread out on the ground with the people looking at and pointing to areas on the map. I sensed words forming for me the idea of mapping "old into new" – as my role.

Journaled on 2/05/06]

I took some time to settle into silence. I asked my questions on my role in Meeting and my role and experience with Quakers. For a long time nothing came. I had some pain in my shoulder from shoveling snow in the morning. After some time, I felt a twinge in my chest on the right [side] curving in an arc about my lung. A feeling sense was slow to develop, but it came as weariness, a sense of tiredness. After sitting with this tiredness, an arc formed on my left side and joined with the right – so that I had two arcs curving down and around coming out on my sides

---

[9] Quakers use the word "Meeting" to refer to their congregation or gathering for worship.

towards my back. Once complete, these arcs formed into chains, and I had a sense of pulling a heavy weight. I looked back and saw a wooden sled piled high with concrete blocks – with Quakers sitting on top. The sled was like those you see in tractor pulling contests. When I looked back the weight on the chain across my chest felt heavier. Then the thought unfolded [for me] we need to find a new way to speak. With this thought the chain lifted, I felt a sense of relief. The Quakers came off the sled. The chain transformed into a flight of geese, each link becoming a bird in a "V" flight honking and trading places in the formation. I felt a sense of lightness and aliveness.

[Journaled on 2/19/06]

I took my time settling into silence. I played with one or two questions, finally letting the question come as "Where do I stand with Quakers now?" My attention turned immediately to my stomach and belly. I could feel my belly [diaphragm] breathing in and out. I felt full with my breathing, but it was constrained and bounded – full and not full at the same time. I stayed with these feelings for a long time. Gradually an image formed around my breathing, an image of a leather bellows moving in and out with my breathing. The leather was old and cracked with cloth patches on it like a sparse patchwork quilt. A thin little tube ran to my heart providing a stream of air to my heart. When I asked, "What does it want me to know?" and "How is it like that?" The answer came as a transformed image as the leather bellows became an organ reaching up and encompassing my heart so that my breathing and heart became one. I felt a relief as the constriction, the boundness, went away. The word "organic" came to me with the image. When I followed by asking, "What is the next step for me?" The answer came clearly – "Start now by writing what you know" where [I understood] the "what you know" meant "know organically." I rested in the knowing.

[Journaled on 4/30/06]

As I settled into silence, a question quickly came to me, "What is my leading in Quakers?" which quickly changed into "What is my leading in life?"[10] I felt a stirring in my heart like life stirring in a cocoon. Quickly an image of a cocoon formed around my heart. The cocoon was wrapped in a cloth shroud. I found myself seated, gently unwrapping the shroud by following instructions in a book – turn a page and unwrap a turn of the shroud. When I asked the questions, "What does it need?" and "What does it want me to know?" The answer came swiftly, "Life is organic" and "The process [understanding] is organic, you can't rush it." I felt a small shift, and easing. My understanding and my leading will unfold.

[Journaled on 6/4/06]

I settled into silence. I set out my question, "What is my leading in Quakers?" And followed with "What is my leading in life?" My attention was drawn quickly to a tug at my heart. I had a feeling sense of anticipation and pain. Words came to me describing the pain as "growing pains." The sense and image of my previous Meditation [on 6/4/06] came to me. The image that formed was a translucent cocoon instead of a shrouded cocoon. Inside was a fetus, which was turning and kicking. Each kick brought a sense of pain. When I asked, "What did I need to know?" and "What was the truth of the situation?" The answer came as "Be prepared" and "Prepare yourself." With this understanding I felt a strong sense of relief. I took the answer to mean to continue my work on understanding, and to be prepared for my leading's "birth" as it would come forward. This meditation had come swiftly. I rested in the silence that followed.

[Journaled on 6/18/06]

---

[10] "Leading" is a Quaker word meaning an inner sense, or an unfolding to undertake a particular course of action.

My Experience

These Light Meditations gave rise to my sense of meaning and direction in writing these Notes. The Meditations arose from my own sense of unease in my role and understanding of life as a Quaker. I am now well into my sixties and I have been an active member of my Quaker Meeting for the last ten years. I was questioning my own life and my life as a Quaker. I was wanting some understanding of both my life and Quaker life.

These Meditations came as a direct experience of "waiting in the light." Each successive Meditation provided an incremental sense of self-understanding, and what I might call "life-understanding." I have often gone back to my sense of the first Meditation where the direction I might take became explicit – "mapping old into new." Have I got that right? Yes, it is old into new. And how might I do *that*? Do it "organically," from my own experiencing. I began these Notes when the direction became clear to me, "Start now by writing what you know." When I tried to rush the writing, my experience in Meditation was not to rush it. The writing and the understanding are part of the same "organic" process. Finally, I have some understanding of the last Meditation. I had expected other Meditations to follow, but my sense of my experience now is that the "birth" in the last Meditation is the unfolding of these Notes. I am writing now from the standpoint of not fully knowing what will come next. I am simply trusting to my direct sense, my direct experience in these Meditations, that what comes will prove right and meaningful for my own life-understanding, and hopefully for your understanding as well.

From a Focusing Point of View

Looking at my Light Meditations from a Focusing point of view, I am quite sure that the sense of inward movement in each Meditation will seem quite familiar to those who have practiced Focusing. While the Meditations employ the symbols of "light" and "truth," I find my felt sense forms in the *same way* as in Focusing.[11] The Meditations show

---

[11] I say the *same way* because I am focusing here on the sameness in the forming of a felt sense. My experience is that Meditation and Focusing are the same *and* different. The situations, the interaction contexts, are different. For example, in

those aspects of bodily sensing, emotional quality, image and words (symbols) usually encountered in forming a felt sense.[12] The Meditations may appear more concise and coherent than a Focusing session. I think this aspect of coherence arises from the additional processing that takes place with journaling. I know many Focusers also journal their Focusing sessions. I would guess that they do so to gain this added coherence, which comes with the distancing provided by journaling.

Forming a Felt Sense

How is it that I know a felt sense has formed? What does the *forming* feel like? First, I find the feeling is different than any other feeling. It has the feel of an interaction, a give and take quality, but the interaction brings me a sense of aliveness as if I were interacting with life itself. I feel fully alive. Second, the forming "comes." The forming takes time. I wait, open, question, and wait. I sense a coming – *when* it comes. This coming is not something I can will, or predict. I often have sat, waiting in silence, and nothing has happened. When a felt sense is forming, I am aware that the process takes time, as if the forming is a *solidifying*. Finally, when a felt sense has solidified, I experience an immense feeling or relief, of satisfaction and joy, as if "things have fallen into place." I have a sense of a next step, a way forward. The step may not be explicit, but I *have* the sense that the step is there.

During the forming of a felt sense, I also have the experience of an expanded sense of self. I have mentioned this understanding as a "self-understanding." This experience comes to me in an odd sort of way. I indicated that the interaction of a felt sense forming has a give and take quality to it. For me, this interaction also has an "over and back" quality where my sense of self has expanded into a new vast space. Going "over" into this space, I have the image that I am a new star exploding into a vast, black space moving past distant star clusters. I am assuming there

---

Focusing the interaction often is pair-wise; in Light Meditation, the interaction is group-wise. These situations are different in that our on-going implying in a situation always includes a sense of others present.

[12] For a brief description of forming a felt sense, see A.W. Cornell, 2005, *The Radical Acceptance of Everything*, pp. 239-242.

is a "back" quality, a coming back because while I have a sense of a new, expanding self, I always come "back" feeling refreshed. I say this experience comes to me in an odd way because I have not journaled this experience directly. When I experience a felt sense forming I am aware of an expanded sense of self, but the sense of "over and back" comes to me as a kind of residual memory. When I return to my journaled Meditations, this memory image of "over and back" is *there* in my sense of self-understanding.

The Felt Sense as a Direct Referent

Gendlin calls the formed felt sense a Direct Referent.[13] By that he means that we can feel, think and act directly from this experience. We can refer directly to our formed felt sense as we seek our way forward. We "have" it, and we can continue to interact with it as we seek the next step, and the next step, and the step after that. Certainly, this is my experience as I have set out these Notes following on from my Meditations. Just as forming a felt sense has a different feel, so too does the referring to the felt sense have a different feel. Using the felt sense from my Meditations as a guide, I have changed my life-situation. The same sense of aliveness and energy that I experienced in Meditation carries forward as I seek to think and act directly from *that* experience. Consider the life-changes that I have made. I have moved from beginning with a sense of despair at understanding my life to set aside a year to study Gendlin's *Process Model*, and added on another year plus to write these Notes as a way of working out my own "life-understanding." At each continuing step, I have had a feeling of the rightness, meaning, and direction of that step – all rolled into one whole. Each step carries me forward, and each step is an unfolding of the whole sequence that carries me forward. This feeling sense of fullness and wholeness leads me to say that I am interacting with my own life implying. In thinking and writing these Notes, I am living that implying. I am carrying my life forward by taking and making each step as it unfolds for me.

---

[13] E. Gendlin, APM, pp. 225-231.

NVC Self-Empathy and Empathy

While I have described and discussed my Meditations from a Quaker and a Focusing point of view, I want to turn now to discuss my Meditations from an NVC point of view. From an NVC viewpoint, I can frame my Meditations as a series of NVC self-empathy sessions.

Self-Empathy

Let's take my first Meditation. Here is a description of that Meditation following the NVC model:

What was I observing about myself? I was uneasy with my role in Quakers. I was dissatisfied with current Quaker thought. I believe current Quaker thought lacks energy and imagination. I was uneasy with my life, thinking that I was lacking meaning and direction.

What was I feeling? I felt a pain in my heart, a weariness and tiredness with Quakers, an aching and a longing for more.

What was I needing? I needed meaning and direction in my role in Quakers and in my life. I needed to understand my own life experiences.

What requests might I make of myself? I asked for a next step. As soon as I asked for the next step, the answer came: map the "old into new." I came alive. I had a felt sense of meaning and direction in my life and my role in Quaker life.

I have set out this description in a shortened way to show that the NVC self-empathy process is an aspect of the same process that we describe as a felt sense forming. We experience a resulting felt shift when we interact with and symbolize our implying in forming a felt sense.

While starting to write these Notes on self-empathy, I went back and re-read Marshall Rosenberg's chapter on self-empathy. I marked out a story, "The Lesson of the Polka-Dotted Suit," which he tells about himself. I have heard him tell this story. It is one of my favorites since I have ruined many new shirts by sticking an uncapped pen in my shirt pocket. In this story Marshall had just purchased a new light gray suit, which he ruined by putting an uncapped pen in his suit pocket while rushing to meet with participants at one of his workshops. After beating himself up about ruining his suit, he gave himself empathy by asking: "What need lies behind my judging myself as 'careless' and 'stupid'?"

> Immediately I saw that it was to take better care of myself: to have given more attention to my own needs while I was rushing to address everyone else's needs. As soon as I touched that part of myself and connected to the deep longing to be more aware and caring of my own needs, *my feelings shifted*. There was a release of tension in my body as the anger, shame, and guilt I was harboring towards myself dissipated. I fully mourned the ruined suit and the uncapped pen as I *opened to feelings* of sadness now arising along with the yearning to take better care of myself.[14]

Here we can see a felt shift occurring, *"my feelings shifted,"* as Marshall connects with his own need to "take better care of himself" – to care for his own needs. "There was a release of tension in my body as the anger… dissipated." Then his feelings shifted again to sadness as he *"opened"* and interacted with his "yearning to take better care" of himself.

I want to explore the relation between needs and implying later. For now I simply want to point to two aspects of the NVC self-empathy process that point to a felt sense forming and an accompanying felt shift. In my own experience, when I connect with my feelings and needs in a situation my feelings and needs are always bodily sensed; they are located in my body. When I turn to connect with my needs, the process is interactive and I am aware that it takes time for my need to form. Once, I have connected with that need, I have a sense of solution and a way forward. More often than not, I can relax. I can feel tension go out of my body.

Empathy

I became acutely aware of looking at NVC needs as symbolizing a felt sense forming when I participated in an empathy training session at an

---

[14] M. Rosenberg, 2003, Op. cit., pp. 134-135. I have added *italics*, marking the feeling shifts.

NVC International Intensive Training (IIT) Workshop that my wife Becky and I attended in Santa Barbara, CA.

I recall the empathy session was about feelings and needs that arise around the issue of money. We participated in the session in groups of three. Each person offered empathy to a partner while the third person observed to make comments in a debriefing afterwards. I partnered by offering empathy (listening, reflecting, and gentle questioning) to a man who set out describing a work situation where his wages were out of line with those offered to a new hire. My partner had been with the company for some time and had inadvertently learned that the newcomer's wages exceeded his own for comparable work. After these observations, we began by looking inward for his feelings:

"And how does that make you feel?"

"I'm angry and upset. I'm frustrated. It's not right." I remember his body tightening up as he spoke.

"So, I hear you say that you're frustrated and angry at the situation."

"Yes! Ummm." He continued to tighten up.

"Can you say where you feel the anger?"

"Right here." He pointed to the center of his chest. "Right here."

"And is there a need there?"

"Yes." After a time, "Yes, respect." After more time, "And understanding, I'm wanting respect and understanding for my work."

"So, you are needing respect and understanding."

"Yes."

"Underneath, is there another need there?"

"Ummmm. Yes." After a long pause, "Ahhhhhh! Fairness… I want fairness."

As soon as he said "Ahhhhhh!" and "Fairness" I saw his body relax, the tension went out of his face. He eased in his chair. I felt my own body relax in response to his easing. At that point I "knew" that I had witnessed a felt sense forming and that a felt shift had occurred. I felt the shift resonate in my own body.

We rested with his need for a time. Then, I asked him whether he wanted to look for a strategy or a request. He said, "No." And after a pause, "I'm OK for now. I can work it out."

In our debriefing that followed, my partner was relaxed. I remember he had a slight smile as he explained that he anticipated he would talk to his boss. He said that he wasn't yet sure what he would say, but he felt confident that he would be able to work out what he would say. In our debriefing I had the sense that we just as easily could have been talking about an experience and realization coming out of a Focusing session.

Getting Beyond Words – Implicit Space

What happens when we interact with our implying? How might we conceptualize a felt sense forming and a Direct Referent arising from that forming? Both my reading of Gendlin's work and my own experience suggest we have something new here – we get beyond words and create a new environment, a new space. I like the term "Implicit Space" for this new space.[15]

In trying to visualize this experience of implicit space, I often visualize geese taking off from a pond. Geese take a few running steps on the water in order to become airborne. Think of our symboling sequences in Meditation (or Focusing, or NVC) as steps we take in symbol space in order to become airborne, to get beyond that space. However, unlike our friends, the geese, we create our implicit space, our new environment, by an inward act of flying. We get beyond words, beyond our situation for a moment, or moments, however fleeting. We experience a life-affirming

---

[15] "Space" here is used in the same way as in symbol space; it is not positional space, rather it is the environment in which we interact. Gendlin has various terms for this new space. The concept of implicit space is laid out in the APM, Chapter VIII-A, pp. 216 – 261.

"Yes! Yes!" moment. Afterwards the outward changes we show may be quite small, as was the case with my workshop friend who showed only a slight smile after our empathy session. The internal changes, however, often are enormous. I think of my own Meditations where what seemed impossible one moment suddenly became possible in the next – "mapping old into new." Is that it? Yes, just *that*. With just *that* I could carry my life-situation forward in a new way.

When we interact with our implying we experience life in this new way. The experience feels different. In Gendlin's terms, we experience a new feel for the whole of our situation. The "whole situation" moves forward. This is the body focaling the implying of the next move.[16]

Our feeling interaction with our implying is our feeling of change as the whole situation "gels" for us. We get both a sense of our life-situation and a way forward. With this opening of a way forward, a new fresh sense of self comes – a new self and a new beginning. This is the change that we "needed" to carry forward.[17]

Leadings

I want to focus on one aspect of the felt sense (the Direct Referent) that forms when we interact with our implying. This is the aspect that Quakers call "leading." Here I am explicitly *mapping* my experiences of the Quaker understanding of "leading" into Gendlin's concept of the Direct Referent.[18]

In my own experience when I wait upon the "promptings of love and truth in my heart" I often am led to change my life in setting upon a new path.[19] For me this aspect of leading, of being led, first arises as a

---

[16] E. Gendlin, APM, p. 223.

[17] Ibid., p. 234.

[18] From an APM standpoint, I am crossing my Quaker experiences of a leading with my understanding of the concept of the Direct Referent.

[19] The quote is from the Quaker Advice: "Take heed, dear Friends, to the promptings of love and truth in your hearts. Trust them as the leadings of God whose Light shows us our darkness and brings us to new life." Britain Yearly Meeting, 1995, *Quaker Faith & Practice*, 2nd Edition, Advices and Queries, 1.02.1.

feeling sense that my life is about-to-change. When I respond by opening to that feeling then a sense of "direction" comes to me. This sense of direction is not just any direction, but it is the "right direction." Following this sense of "right direction" leads me to change, to a new beginning, to a new course of action.

The series of five Meditations, which form the basis for these Notes, are in my Quaker experience a *leading*. In my fourth Meditation,[20] I already had a strong sense of my-life-is-about-to-change and explicitly asked, "What is my leading in life?" The answer came as a further sense of "direction" that "life is organic" and "will unfold." I am following *that* leading in writing these Notes.

Gendlin makes the same point with regards to a formed felt sense, a Direct Referent. When a Direct Referent has formed, we have a feeling sense of "direction."[21] This "direction" has no explicit content, no explicit form; yet we "know" that we have a direction. This direction is still implicit, still to unfold. In my own case, this feeling sense of "right direction" only took an explicit form as a course of action when I set out to write these Notes.

I can say then from my own experience,

A Quaker leading is a formed felt sense, a Direct Referent, or at least that aspect of a Direct Referent that gives rise to a sense of right direction to carry life forward in a new way.[22]

What then? What do we do after we have a Direct Referent? We have to work it out in symbol space. We have to live out our leading in symbol space.

---

[20] On p. 58.

[21] E. Gendlin, APM, p. 250.

[22] I say "at least" because I think that Direct Referent is both a more complex and more precise concept than leading.

Speaking in a New Way

Ah! If we only lived in implicit space, how sweet it might be. However, we live in symbol space and we must work out what to say and do. We do that by referring to our experience formed in implicit space. This experience is our reference (Direct Referent), our feeling sense that brings forth words and actions. I write this sentence now as I am checking inside to see how I might express that we speak and act in a new way when we "have" a Direct Referent. When I "touch" my Direct Referent, the sentence comes again,

A Quaker leading is a formed felt sense, a Direct Referent, or at least that aspect of a Direct Referent that gives rise to a sense of right direction to carry life forward in a new way.

This is an entirely new sentence written (and spoken) in a new way. I had never seen, heard, or thought of this sentence before writing it (above). I wrote it this second time just to make the point that this is a *new* sentence; that *I am speaking about my Quaker experience in a new way.* This sentence expresses an aliveness within me that carries forward my felt sense from my Meditations and transforms (deepens) my understanding of a Quaker leading. I wrote the sentence by going inside, opening to my felt sense (my Direct Referent formed in Meditation) and letting the sentence "come" to me.

Gendlin calls this working out "second sequences."[23] These second sequences are words (and actions), which are implicit in a Direct Referent. We work out how we will speak and act out of our experience by interacting with a formed felt sense, a Direct Referent. Each interaction is new and carries us forward.[24] I like to think of this working out as the ripples spreading out in a pond after a stone has disturbed the surface. Each ripple interaction is a freeing, a lifting up with life moving on and out from a new center.

---

[23] Ibid., pp. 245-246. The "first sequence" is the forming of the felt sense (Direct Referent) in implicit space.

[24] In Quaker practice, we use the term "testing" to describe working out a leading.

Sitting with this initial understanding of *working out* has brought an answer to a question that has puzzled me for some time:

How can a single experience, a single instance, change and transform a life and the lives of others?

I find the answer straightforward:

A singular experience of a formed felt sense arising from interacting with our implying applies to *everything*.[25]

Everything refers to all the instances, which we may work out by making explicit the second sequences, the sequences of words and actions, implicit in the Direct Referent. Each time we work out a sequence (in symbol space), we carry our life (and the Direct Referent) forward. Each instance is, in effect, a new expression, a new carrying forward. Each instance changes the context in which we act and live within symbol space, including our interactions with others.

What we experience, what I have experienced as I work out from my Direct Referent here, is a great inner sense of power to speak (and act). This power comes, I think, from the sense of freedom, of release from speaking and acting within a life-situation. Suddenly, when we "touch" a Direct Referent, we are outside our situation; we can think, act and speak clearly. Words come freshly, or if we speak old words they have new meanings and new power. Words come alive, and resonate when we speak with others. As we speak and act to carry our life forward, our speaking and acting can resonate with others who seek to change or want to change their own life-situation (or their own life-understanding), and likely (I suspect) with others who have yet to express a need for change.

---

[25] Gendlin calls one form of this working out process *monading*. He uses the expression, "…a Direct Referent 'monads out into everything'" in APM, p. 246. See also pp. 263-270.

Holding and Letting[26]

I want to return now to our process question and pull together my understanding of how symbol sequences provide for personal change and transformation.

Our question was,

"How is it possible to use words to learn to get beyond words in order to speak (use) words in a new way?"

While each of the language (symbol) sequences that we learn to use to initiate change in our practice (Quaker, Focusing, or NVC) may seem at first complex (four or six steps) and diverse in the choice of words,[27] the basic change process is simple and common to each practice.

I can say,

We can change our lives when we hold a situation in symbol space and let a felt sense form in a new space, implicit space. Holding and letting is our interacting with our implying. Once a felt sense has formed, we can then "work out" what to say or do in symbol space to further carry our lives forward.

Holding and letting is one activity, one process. By engaging in a symboling (language) sequence we intend to hold a situation, to keep the point of our concern, problem, or conflict, and let change come as a felt sense forms. This process takes time. It may take a few seconds or, as in the case of my Meditations, it may take months.

I say *can* change because a felt sense forms only when it forms. Despite our best intentions and our familiarity with engaging in a symboling sequence, a felt sense may not come, or if it comes it often is not what we expected. Each felt sense is a singular experience and has its own character.

---

[26] E. Gendlin, APM, p. 233.

[27] Table – Language Sequences, p. 52.

My saying that holding and letting is one process does not make the process any easier. We live in symbol space, within situations with thinned emotions and too complex roles. It is not easy to hold in symbol space. Holding means not moving forward by speaking words, or acting or feeling the way we think we "should" act and feel. As soon as we turn inward we turn over the discomfort, pain, fear and disconnect in our lives. Holding often means holding pain. It is easy to turn away and to try to "slide by."

If we hold and let a felt sense form, then we get beyond our situation. We get beyond the words that we have used that failed to carry us forward. Once a felt sense has formed we *can* speak and act in a new way. All the contexts in symbol space have crossed, and we "have" a new reference, a new center. The felt sense is a *focaled* way forward, a new way because we have a reference "outside" our situation.

I say we *can* speak and act in a new way. I don't say that we will. We still live in symbol space. We still have to work things out. Working out is not easy. I do not mean to imply that having a Direct Referent means that everything will fall into place without effort. As I write this I am thinking of a past Meditation where a felt sense formed. I had a clear leading, a clear realization of what steps I might take. I choose not to take those steps, or rather I let too much time pass before the situation changed and was out of my hands. The situation is still too painful for me to recount the details here. I can say then from my own experience that we can turn away from a formed felt sense. When we do, the sense fades over time and we are left with regret and pain.

Light and Truth

If holding and letting is the basic process that we seek, how then does the Quaker process employing light and truth map into occurring into implying? How does the "old map into the new"?

If we "wait in the light" or "turn to the light" or "hold in the light" what we are doing is holding and letting, we are seeking to interact with our implying.

I can say then from my own experience and understanding,

Light is implying. Or, light is another way of symbolizing implying.

If we wait upon our implying, what comes is the truth.

Again, I can say from my own experience,

Truth is what carries life forward. Or, truth is another way of symbolizing what carries life forward.

Truth is implicit and explicit. It is both our on-going implying to carry life forward, and what we say or do explicitly (when we interact with our implying) to carry life forward. In this sense, truth is always present for us if we choose to live it.

Early on I marked out a Quaker-like quote from Gendlin that I liked and wanted to use to make this point about implicit/explicit truth. Here is the quote:

> What is true is already so. Owning up to it doesn't make it worse. Not being open to it doesn't make it go away. And because it is true, it is there to be interacted with. Anything untrue isn't there to be lived. People can stand what is true, for they are already enduring it.[28]

There is always "more" to the truth than we can say or do in any given moment.[29]

Understanding Fox in a New Way

When I set out to "map" our old Quaker practice of "waiting in the light" into a new experiential form, I had no idea how the "mapping" would sort out. I think I anticipated that the explication would be lengthy and complex. Remarkably, as soon as I understood "holding and

---

[28] E. Gendlin, 1981, *Focusing*, p. 140.

[29] Saying that light symbolizes implying, and truth symbolizes what carries life forward does not preclude or take away from symbolizing an experience with "light" and "truth" as a religious experience. George Fox, of course, wrote and spoke of his experience of the inward light as the "pure light of God."

letting" (above) as an experiential inward turning that we Quakers call "waiting in the light" or "turning to the light," then understanding our Quaker "light" as a way of symbolizing "implying" and our Quaker "truth" as "carrying life forward" quickly fell into place.

With this understanding (crossing) of Quaker "waiting" and "holding and letting" I want to look again, in a modern experiential way, at what George Fox is saying. Consider the following passage from Fox, which I quoted early on in these Notes:

> So long as you live in the light nothing can trip you up, because you will see everything in the light. Do you love the light? Then here's your teacher! When you are walking it's there with you, in your heart – you don't have to say 'Look over here,' 'Look over there.' And as you lie in bed it is there with you too, teaching you, making you aware of that wandering mind of yours that likes to wander off, and of your attempts to master everything with your own thought and imagination – they themselves are mastered by the light.[30]

Now, we can understand why Fox says the "light" is always with us. Our on-going implying is always with us, we have only to turn and wait, the "truth" will come to us; what will carry life forward comes to us. Life itself is our teacher! When we form a felt sense out of our on-going implying, we touch the stream of life, we touch life itself. This felt experiencing does not come from our "wandering mind," rather it comes in and from the "heart." Our living is an embodied process. When we "live in the light," we turn and live into our own implying to change. Each step forward is a turning to, speaking into, and acting into the intricacy of our own implying; and there is always "more" to our living, more to come, more to understand, to speak, and to do.

What Do We Gain?

As Quakers, what do we gain by understanding Fox in this modern experiential way? What we *regain*, I think, is a clearer understanding

---

[30] George Fox in R. Ambler, 2002, Op. cit., p. 8, and quoted on p. 7 of these Notes.

that our living, and our Quaker practice, is an embodied process, an in-the-body-curl-your-toes process. (We "quake" because we come alive as we turn and open into implicit space to speak.) We also gain a clearer understanding of how change and transformation come to us. When we get "beyond words" and form a felt sense in implicit space, we get beyond our situation and form a new center, a Direct Referent that leads us to speak and act in a changed way. We "work out" our change as we carry our living forward in symbol space. I think this understanding of "working out" from a Direct Referent gives us a more precise way of thinking about how our Quaker leadings work. Most importantly, I think that understanding Fox in this experiential way gives us another way, a new way, to speak to others about our Quaker practice. We can, if we choose, speak to others in a new "language." For many moderns, the Quaker sense of "light" and "truth" has no resonance, and no meaning. We can, if we choose, speak to others in this more modern experiential idiom. It will help us in these times, I think, to have a second language to speak about our Quaker practice.

What are we to make now of Fox's phrase "mastered by the light"? Here, I think we gain a new understanding of what it means to think out of our felt experiencing. We can think directly from our own experiencing. Thinking from and out of a felt sense is *an explicit embodied way of thinking*.[31] These Notes are an example of my explicit thinking out (working out) of a Direct Referent formed in Light Meditation. This working out is more than Fox's "mastering" our thinking mind, our now usual disembodied way of thinking. Conceptualizing from and out of a Direct Referent is, in effect, a different way of thinking, and a different way of thinking about thinking. We now have the understanding that when we form a Direct Referent, it is a singular event and we regenerate time and (symbol) space relationships. When we think out of and refer to a Direct Referent, we "work out" our felt meaning of these changed relationships as they apply to *everything* in our living. When we think in this way, we are both thinking from and out of the intricacy of our own

---

[31] This is not meant as a vague reference. Please see the process called "Thinking at the Edge" (TAE) given below in the section on "Thinking about NVC."

living. In this sense, we can give new meaning to Fox's "mastering" as a choosing to both see and think in the light.

Finally, as Quakers let us not forget that our "turning to the light," our "working out" of living in the light is "the first step towards peace."[32]

Non-Violence and NVC

I have brought this thought of peace forward because I want to turn now to look at and talk about non-violence from a process point of view. I want to take our discussion to a point of understanding that

A fully non-violent solution to a conflict situation arises when a felt sense forms in that situation.

In order to reach such an understanding, I need to provide some background about my own work with non-violence, and to establish the context in which I will be talking about non-violence and NVC.

AVP

For the last five years I have facilitated non-violence in the Nevada prison system. I am one member of a team facilitating Alternatives to Violence Project (AVP) Workshops at the Nevada State Prison (NSP), a medium security men's prison in Carson City, NV. AVP was formed in 1975 in Green Haven Prison in New York when a group of inmates asked a local Quaker group for help in putting together a workshop program to facilitate non-violence among youthful offenders. While originally a Quaker program, AVP has been "released" from Quaker oversight and is now organized as an all-volunteer, non-profit educational program. AVP has grown into a multi-cultural national and international program offering workshops in prisons (and communities) in 40 states, and in more than 20 countries.

An AVP workshop is an experiential learning process. Each workshop is three-days (21 hours) long. The exercises, which make up an AVP

---

[32] George Fox in R. Ambler, 2002, Ibid., p. 20, and quoted on p. 5 of these Notes.

workshop, focus on sharing life-experiences, and draw on a broad range of learning skills. In our Advance AVP Workshops on Communication I use some NVC exercises. My workshop experience with using NVC comes then from using a few NVC exercises as a supplement to a larger group of AVP exercises to facilitate non-violence.[33] By design, AVP workshops provide for a complex workshop environment.[34]

The personal changes and transformations that we see in inmate workshop participants are quite extraordinary. We see, for example, changes in self-respect, in communication skills, in learning to relate to other people, and in understanding that each life situation provides for choice and responsibility. By far the most important change which we see is the realization that change itself is possible – that "I can change." For those of you who are unfamiliar with AVP, or who would like to learn more about the AVP process, please take a look at a review report on our AVP work at the men's prison (NSP).[35]

Transforming Power[36]

Later on in the discussion of non-violence that follows I want to make use of one of AVP's organizing ideas. In AVP, we call an Ah! Ha! Moment (the transforming felt shift in a person or situation) a "Transforming Moment," and we call the surge of energy that comes

---

[33] NVC is slowly working its way into prison systems. The Bay Area NVC group has an on-going NVC program in San Quentin Prison, CA. I also understand that Lucy Leu and her co-workers have created, and will release, a new book of NVC exercise based in part on their work in prisons in Seattle, WA, and in Vancouver, BC.

[34] In my experience, one of the main differences between AVP and NVC (and Focusing) is that AVP workshops facilitate personal change *and* community change at the same time. Communities also form around both NVC and Focusing workshops. I think the difference is one of workshop emphasis and intent. Making fundamental life changes without personal support and interaction is extremely difficult. Within the prison yard where AVP operates there is no on-going community to support life-style changes. AVP workshop agendas are designed to build that community from scratch within the prison yard.

[35] H. Rice, 2007, *Review Report on AVP Workshops at Nevada State Prison (NSP)*, available on-line at www.renofriends.org/avp.html.

[36] AVP/USA, 2002, *Alternatives to Violence Project Basic Course Manual*, pp. B-2 – B-11.

with and follows from such a moment "Transforming Power."[37] The idea of Transforming Power comes from the Quaker experience of acting non-violently when faced with violence. For example, many of the Quaker facilitators who helped start AVP had experience in non-violent direct actions in the Civil Rights Movement in the South. A common experience in using non-violence is the experience of an inner sense of power to act in violent confrontations. When confronted with violence, what to say or do "comes" in a Transforming Moment to change or alter the situation in a non-violent way. This experience of the early facilitators has carried over into the basic design of AVP.

In AVP we introduce Transforming Power in the form of a mandala.[38] When the elements in the mandala are present in a situation we teach that we may then expect to experience "an inner sense of power to act." Transforming Power refers to this inner sense of power to act. During the course of our workshops, or in debriefings with inmate facilitators, we hear directly about Transforming Power experiences. Many of our inmate participants tell stories of Transforming Power in "talking down" violent confrontations on the yard.[39] As I write, I am thinking of one specific situation where one of our AVP inmate facilitators intervened to save a young inmate from being continually raped. Given the culture on the prison yard never to interfere in another inmate's affairs, his intervention was an extraordinary act of courage. It took courage not only to intervene, but to do so in a non-violent way that settled the young inmate's accounts with other inmates "whom he owed" so that the situation was ended.

---

[37] A similar phrase to Transforming Power used by Marshall Rosenberg in NVC is "divine energy."

[38] The center is Transforming Power; the inner ring is Respect for Self and Care for Others; the outer ring is Think Before Reacting, Expect the Best, and Reach for a Non-violent Solution.

[39] Some of these situations are attempts to "test" an inmate's commitment to AVP by attempting to provoke a violent response. As one AVP inmate facilitator said, "Doing AVP is like painting a target on your back."

NVC

I have chosen to use NVC as a non-violent practice for these Notes because my experience is that it, like AVP, leads to personal growth, change and transformation. From a process point of view, NVC has the additional advantages that (a) it offers a clear concise model of non-violent communication, and (b) it is taught as a four-step (symboling) sequence. Recall that these four steps are: (1) making an observation about a situation, (2) saying how you feel, (3) identifying and saying your need in the situation, and (4) making a request based on your need. In dialogue form, the same four-step process is used to elicit an understanding of the other person's observations, feelings, needs, and to offer a request (solution) based on your own *and* the other person's needs.[40]

Violence Arises from Unmet Human Needs

I think one important insight offered by Marshall Rosenberg in NVC is the understanding that violence arises from unmet (and often unexpressed) human needs.[41] In this sense, "unmet needs" is another way of saying we are "stuck" in and cannot "meet" a situation. We use this insight of unmet needs in our Basic AVP Workshop in an exercise called "Choices" where we explore the roots and fruits of violence. When we look at needs as forming the roots of violence (and non-violence), we see that violence is a strategy for getting (demanding) that our needs are met in a situation. Alternatively, non-violence is a strategy for meeting those same needs in a life-preserving and life-enriching way. We justify our use of violence by making judgments, criticisms, diagnoses, and interpretations of others. In NVC, Marshall calls these judgments "alienated expressions of our own unmet needs."[42] Violence comes from how we choose to respond to our needs (and feelings) in a situation.

With this background in hand, let's turn to thinking about NVC.

---

[40] See Table of Language Sequences on p. 52.

[41] By needs we mean: autonomy, celebration, integrity, interdependence, play, spiritual communion, and physical nurturance. For a list of needs, please see M. Rosenberg, 2003, Op cit., pp. 54-55.

[42] Ibid., p. 52.

Thinking about NVC

Besides giving Focusing to us as a way to seek a felt sense, Gene Gendlin together with Mary Hendricks also have given us a systematic way to think further from a felt sense. They call this process "Thinking at the Edge" (TAE).[43]

In Appendix B, I describe working through the first five steps in TAE using my felt sense of NVC that formed in my empathy session about money. In the discussion that follows I am going to start from a TAE sentence, which is the last sentence in Appendix B.[44]

Understanding that feelings/needs are aspects of interacting with an implying lets a felt sense form more easily/ accessibly/ simply/ openly/ expressively…in the NVC process.

Understanding Needs in NVC

What do I mean when I say, "that feelings/needs are aspects of interacting with an implying" in the NVC process?

I mean that the words "feelings/needs" perform the same *function* in NVC that they perform in any symboling sequence (like Focusing) that lets a felt sense form. When we say, "What am I feeling?" and "What am I needing?" (Or "What are you feeling?" and "What are you needing?"), I can say,

We are intending to hold to a conflict in symbol space to let a solution form as a felt sense in implicit space.

I am making my understanding of NVC more explicit by conceptualizing "interacting" as "holding and letting." Holding and letting is one activity. In the context of the NVC process, holding and letting means our intent is to hold the conflict (the pattern of words and

---

[43] E. Gendlin and M. Hendricks, 2004, Thinking at the Edge, TAE, pp. 1-24. Steps One through Five are called "Speaking from the Felt Sense."

[44] My empathy session in NVC is on pp. 63-65. If you would like to look at the steps in developing the TAE sentence, please see Appendix B. I have added the words "interacting with" to the TAE sentence in Appendix B to reflect my current thinking in these Notes.

actions) and to let a felt sense form from our implying in the situation. We form a felt sense by bodily sensing our feelings and needs in the situation, and expressing those feelings and needs. In a conflict situation, a formed felt sense will include a sense of the other person and his or her needs. A formed felt sense is a sense of the situation, and the next step forward (a request) to fulfill the expressed needs. In NVC, the forming of the felt sense already includes *care* for the other person. Understanding that a felt sense can (and does) form in the NVC process enables us to cross NVC and Focusing processes. We can experiment with (and experience) how one practice may enhance the other.

Needs Are Not Fixed

The NVC model form suggests feelings cause needs ("... because I am needing").[45] When we look at NVC from this process model point of view, we have a different view of "feelings" and "needs." From a language process point of view,

Needs are not fixed, and the relationship between feelings and needs is not fixed.

I can, for example, say,

"I am feeling tired because I need some rest."

Or, I can say,

"I need some rest because I am feeling tired."

From a process standpoint there is no reason to give preference to one form of saying over the other. I think viewing feelings and needs as having a fixed causal relationship ("because") may limit letting a felt sense form. Both are aspects of forming a felt sense.[46] I think it better serves the change process just to say, "I am feeling" *and* "I am needing." Why limit the process by assuming a fixed (causal) relationship?

---

[45] See Language Table on p. 52.

[46] A feeling sense is the central point in any symbolizing interaction. We have a feeling sense and we find (fit) a word "need" to symbolize what we mean. Here we find (symbolize) a "need" to carry us forward. See the discussion on symbolizing meaning on pp. 30-33.

Thinking that feelings and needs have a fixed causal relationship may do more than limit the solution process. In some (rare) instances, I think it is possible that this assuming may actually contribute to forming a block to letting a felt sense form. I have observed (and am now reflecting on) situations in NVC workshops where a solution (a felt sense) failed to form during an NVC empathy session. It is, of course, not possible to say completely why a solution failed to form. However, I am thinking now of a particular instance where a young woman got part way though an NVC empathy "healing" session only to stop in tears, and to keep repeating over and over again something like, "I am feeling afraid because I am needing money and support for my NVC work." She was unable to move beyond that point, despite repeated attempts to help her "reframe" her thinking.

Because that instance troubled me greatly at the time, I have carried it forward. I am struck now (as I think about it) by the similarity to Gendlin's discussion of "analysis" as a block in Focusing, where repeating an analysis does nothing to move the inner process forward.[47] In this case, the young woman's "analysis" may have been quite correct, but it did nothing to touch her discomfort and pain. I believe she slipped into a "because," got stuck, and could not move beyond to get in touch with the intricacy of her own implying and let a felt sense form that would carry her forward.

In thinking more about "needs," let's consider the following example where a couple, Jack and Jill, are on the verge of an argument over how to spend their Saturday.

Jill says, "Jack I need your help this morning turning over the garden so that I can plant my flowers."

Jack responds, "Maybe later. Right now I'm just beat. I just need some time and space to unwind from work."

"Jack you promised. I need your help. I love my garden. It's my joy."

---

[47] See page 15. The Focusing reference is E. Gendlin, 1981, Op. cit., pp. 36-37.

"I know dear, but I just need to unwind."

"You promised. Please don't put me off. I need your help."

Jack pauses for a moment and says, "Ummmm ... Honey, Let's go for a hike in the mountains."

"Oh, Jack! You're just putting me off again."

"No, I'm serious. I want to go to the mountains. The spring flowers are out. We missed them last year and the year before. Let's not miss them again!... Let's just pick up and go."

"Jack, I'd like to go, but I need to get my planting done."

"I could take two or three hours tomorrow, and do enough to get you started. We could do the rest during the week."

"Jack, please don't make another promise that you won't keep."

"I will do it tomorrow morning! I'm willing to do it tomorrow. Please, let's pick up and go."

After her own pause, Jill responds, "OK, let's go!"

Of course, Jack and Jill spent the day happily hiking in the mountains among the spring wild flowers.

In this example, what needs were met with the solution to go hiking? It is possible that hiking met Jack's expressed need to unwind, and also met Jill's need (and love) for flowers. The situation is ambiguous. The solution to go hiking just comes out of a pause. It is equally possible that getting away and hiking met an unexpressed need for Jack and Jill to be together and to share an activity they both like. Of course, I get to say (because I made up the example) that Jill and Jack came to realize that they needed the time and joy of being together among the spring flowers. We only "know" the *relevant* need after we meet (and carry forward) the situation.

The point I want to make here is that needs are not fixed. Needs are not predetermined possibilities that we find and fulfill in a present situation. When a felt sense forms everything crosses with everything in the present. All "past" and "future" needs are crossed and focaled to the need in the present situation. A felt sense, as it forms, is usually vague at first. It solidifies as we seek to find the word "need" that fits. We experience this "solidifying" as a series of feeling shifts as "words" come to us, and we interact with our implying until we have a "word" fit. This need often is our expressed need (and the other person's expressed need), but it may be an unexpressed need and come as a surprise, "Oh, *that* need!" This is the need that we had set aside, or the need that we had avoided. A formed felt sense is the symbolized need, the next step forward and the solution to the conflict. A need forms as a felt sense only as it can form. It is, as we might say in other times, a matter of "grace."

It is just this (above) understanding that feelings/needs are aspects of interacting with an implying that leads me to say that this understanding,

Lets a felt sense form more easily/ accessibly/ simply/ openly/ expressively…in the NVC process.

Using NVC Exercises to Facilitate a Felt Sense

If the underlying change process in Focusing and in NVC is the same process, then it should be possible to use NVC exercises to facilitate forming a felt sense. I find this is the case. After some trial and error in my prison work, I have settled on using a form of an NVC "Empathy Exercise" to facilitate experiencing a bodily felt sense and felt shift.

In the exercise form that I use,[48] two facilitators model letting a felt sense form by recalling and working with two situations. The first is a situation where a need was met, and the second is a situation where a need was unmet. The facilitators take turns working with each situation. The process starts with the active facilitator briefly describing the situation he or she is going to use. (The fewer words the better to avoid

---

[48] I learned the exercise that I use from Meganwind Eoyang. We commonly use past situations, but some participants elect to use present situations. This exercise works along the same line as the empathy sequence that I described on pp. 63-65.

any narrative.) The second person provides empathy by listening and reflecting as the active person reports first on his or her feelings, locating the bodily sense of the feelings, and then the bodily sensed needs associated with those feelings. Both feelings and needs may shift until the person comes to "rest" with one need. When the person comes to "rest" there is a palpable felt shift. You can see the felt shift occur as the body eases, color comes to the face, and breathing deepens and slows as relief comes. Some NVC facilitators call this extended moment "resting in the beauty of the need."

After modeling the process, we do the exercise by pairing participants. We work with twenty inmate participants so we usually are working with ten pairs (or twelve pairs if facilitators join in). Each participant takes a turn at working with each situation. The responses that I see in this exercise are extraordinary. Almost all the participants experience a felt shift. Not experiencing a felt shift is the exception. There is an audible hush and hum in the room as feelings ebb and flow. Many of the participants are working with excruciatingly painful situations when a need was unmet, and find this empathy exercise a deeply moving experience

The Illusion of Conflicting Needs

Another NVC exercise that I like is called "The Illusion of Conflicting Needs."[49] This is not an exercise that I use in prison, but I have used it in community workshops and informally with friends. I particularly like this exercise (and include it here) because it provides a simple way to experience the body *focaling* a "need." This exercise makes use of the fact that we commonly make many of our daily decisions using a felt sense.[50] We usually are not aware that we are making decisions in this

---

[49] I learned this NVC exercise from Robert Gonzales at the IIT workshop in Santa Barbara, CA. Robert calls the process experienced in this exercise, "the living energy of needs." For a more complete description and explanation of this exercise, please contact Robert at his website, www.living-compassion.org.

[50] On average we make about 200 decisions a day. We make many of these decisions unknowingly with a felt sense, as when we "sleep on it." I learned this estimate of 200 from an inmate who had researched the topic. I don't have any reason to doubt the number. By contrast, the average inmate makes at most twenty decisions a day.

way. This NVC exercise makes our choice process explicit by focusing on the feelings and needs of alternative steps.

To work with this exercise you need a situation where you are faced with, or are considering a choice between two conflicting needs or next steps. I think it works best with a present situation, say something like two options in a work situation. I will describe the exercise as you might do it alone in a self-empathy session, but the exercise can be done pair-wise as an empathy session where your companion offers empathy by listening and reflecting as you relate your sensing process.

To do the exercise, seat yourself on a straight back chair, or any chair without arm rests. Close our eyes, get comfortable, and relax. Let your arms hang down at your sides, then turn your palms until they face forward. Keep your upper arms close to you body, and slowly flex your forearms until they are horizontal. You want to end up in a position with your forearms extended with the palms up as if you were holding a small soft pillow in each hand.

When you are ready, visualize placing one alternative in your left hand and the other in your right hand.[51] This is meant (and explained) as a purely symbolic act, and not an energetic act. Now beginning with either hand ask yourself (and bodily sense) what you are feeling and needing with this choice. Then, turn your attention to the other hand and ask what you are feeling and needing with that choice. Repeat the process by going back and forth asking after feelings and needs for each choice until you have a clear bodily sensed need for each choice. Focus on each need, and then bring both needs into your awareness at the same time. Hold both needs in your awareness, and let a felt sense of the whole of your needs form. As you hold both needs in your awareness, you may shift from one need to the other, or you may hold both in you awareness at the same time. As a felt sense "gels," one hand likely will slowly sink as if under an

---

[51] I don't think the assigning matters. My own experience is that a felt sense forming overcomes any sense of handedness. Assigning options or choices to the hands is meant as an aid in learning the exercise. Once learned, the exercise is easily done without using the hands. If you are an experienced Focuser trying this exercise, you may find the hands a distraction!

increasing weight, and the other hand will rise. Alternatively, one or both choices may change in the process and a new choice may present itself. When carried to completion your awareness will be drawn to the weighted hand whether this is an original choice, or a new changed choice and next step. The weighted hand is the body *focaling* the need and the next step. The apparent conflict in "needs" falls away with the focaling.

Hard to Hear Messages

Now, I would like to turn and relate an experience with another NVC exercise called "Hard to Hear Messages." This exercise is based on the chapter in Marshall's book called "Taking Responsibility For Our Feelings."[52] The exercise involves practicing four ways to respond when hearing a negative message. The four ways are: (1) blaming ourselves; (2) blaming others; (3) sensing our own feelings and needs; and (4) sensing others' feelings and needs. The last two options call for practicing NVC.

The time I am recalling was a time when we did the exercise in an Advanced AVP Communication prison workshop just after I had started to play with the idea that a felt sense forms in NVC. I had set out to model the exercise with another facilitator, Marc, our lead inmate facilitator. Marc and I had gone over the exercise several times in our planning for the workshop. In modeling the exercise one facilitator says a hard-to-hear message, and the second person responds by answering. The exercise calls for working progressively through the four options using the same message each time. I can't remember the exact wording of the hard-to-hear-message that we had agreed Marc would give me to start the dialogue sequence. I know that it had something to do with my inclination for watching the workshop clock and trying to keep our workshop agenda on track. I remember the words, "control freak." So, I'm guessing the dialogue sequence started with Marc saying something like,

"You're a complete control freak. All you do is watch the clock! You don't see what's actually going on around you."

---

[52] M. Rosenberg, 2003, Op. cit., pp. 49-50.

I responded and we got through modeling the first two blaming responses.

Then for some reason as we started to model the first NVC response, rather than respond by looking inward for my feelings and needs in the situation, I turned (unthinkingly) inward and waited for a felt sense to form as I might in Meditation. Some time must have passed because Marc interrupted my reverie by asking,

"What's going on?"

I blurted out, "I'm waiting for a felt sense to form!"

My response caught Marc off-guard because we had not talked about a felt sense in our exercise planning. I am sure he had no idea what I was talking about. However, Marc is quick, and he responded without missing a beat by saying,

"While we're waiting for your felt sense the guys could have had a break with two smokes by now!"

I got flustered and I'm sure I went completely red-faced. But, Marc's comment brought me back to the situation. He eased me gently back into the situation by asking,

"Are you OK?"

I answered, "Yes, I'm OK." And something like, "I lost my way for a moment."

As we went on with the exercise, I regained my composure. I was able to establish an empathetic connection with Marc, made easier by the gentle and caring way he brought me back to the situation. I then was able to connect with and express my feelings of frustration and my need for understanding. Marc listened to me and we were able to move on and complete modeling an NVC dialogue.

What Happened?

I tell this story with some amusement now, but at the time I was mortified. When I reflect back on my experience, I see that I was so taken with the notion that a felt sense forms in NVC that I forgot that the first response in NVC dialogue (or any dialogue) is to provide empathy. By turning inward in my usual way for Meditation to let a felt sense form, I failed to provide any response at all, let alone an empathetic response. I simply had turned away from the situation.

What I take away from this experience is the understanding that dialogue is different. It is, of course, a different situation, a different interaction context than we encounter in Focusing and Meditation. Focusing and Meditation usually take place in an empathetic situation. When we are in a conflict situation, we often have someone "in our face." Using a computer metaphor, I like to think of Focusing and Meditation as off-line activities, and dialogue as an on-line activity. I say on-line activity because the key difference is:

When we are in a conflict dialogue we are actively in the symboling pattern (words and actions), which we are trying to change.

Pausing Is a Different Activity[53]

I think the key to understanding a non-violent dialogue form, like NVC, is to understand that

We need to pause the pattern of words and actions in order to let a felt sense form. We need to pause the pattern while we are in the pattern.

The intent to let a felt sense form is the same as in Focusing (or Meditation), but the activity of "pausing" when we engage in dialogue is different. If we do not "pause" the pattern, which constitutes the situation we are in, then the pattern will carry forward and we will continue the conflict, repeating what we have said and done before. Pausing lets a felt sense form beyond the pattern, and provides us with a solution to carry the situation forward in a new way.

---

[53] E. Gendlin, APM, p. 229. I am using "pausing" here to mean, "pausing and letting."

Let's turn now to look at NVC dialogue from a process model point of view. I think Marshall Rosenberg offers three key insights, which contribute immeasurably to "pausing" a conflict situation, and letting a felt sense form. These three insights are:

1. Putting feelings and needs in a symmetrical dialogue form.[54] Other non-violent practices, like AVP, recognize and teach expressing feelings and needs, but usually do so only from the speaker's point of view. I think putting dialogue in a symmetrical form (seeking needs for both persons) facilitates letting a felt sense form from the expressed needs.

2. Making non-judgmental observations about the conflict situation. More often than not, a conflict starts with and includes a disagreement about the situation itself. Making non-judgmental observations helps shape the front end of a dialogue.

3. Making requests in a positive doable form. Even after a solution has formed in a dialogue situation we still have to "work it out." Helping shape the form of the request in a non-violent way increases the chances that a solution will be carried through.[55]

In the discussion that follows, I will work through the NVC dialogue sequence by commenting on these three elements, and on what I see as differences between "pausing" in dialogue and in "off-line" activities, like Focusing.

Empathy First

In a conflict dialogue, we start with empathy. By empathy I mean a willingness to be with the other person in the situation, *and* a willingness to be with your self in the situation. Dialogue requires both empathy and self-empathy. Ask yourself, "Are you willing to be with the other person in this situation?" If not, then nothing is going to happen. Starting with

---

[54] See the NVC dialogue in the Language Table on p. 52.

[55] Added Note. NVC empathy and self-empathy are practiced in the same form ("What am I feeling?" and "What am I needing?") as the dialogue form. I think these NVC practices make the transition to dialogue ("on-line") much easier.

empathy is common to any situation where we seek to carry life forward. Establishing an empathetic connection in dialogue is more difficult because we need to maintain a balance between providing empathy to the other person and providing empathy to our self. If we turn away then we lose the empathetic connection. If we fail to maintain self-empathy, then we can "lose our selves in the situation."

Breaking Patterns by Observing without Evaluating[56]

When we engage in Focusing or Meditation, we are intending to break thinking and language patterns that block our moving forward. The same holds true in a dialogue situation. In NVC, we start breaking the pattern by making "vanilla" observations about the situation, consciously avoiding the "shoulds," "demands," "blaming," and "judgments" that help make up the conflict situation. Starting to break the word patterns describing the situation helps lead to a common understanding of the situation itself.

Seeking Common Ground

In NVC dialogue, the core activity is revealing our own feelings and our needs in the situation, and seeking to elicit and understand the other person's feelings and needs. We understand the other's feelings and needs by listening and reflecting, gentle questioning, and more listening and reflecting until we fully understand what the other person has said. Understanding in this way provides the other with an affirmation that he or she has been heard. We reveal our own feelings and needs in the same way until we are certain that we have been heard. Affirming the other person and having our own expressions affirmed doesn't necessarily mean that we have reached a solution. It only means that we have reached a common ground where each of us has had our feelings and needs heard, and that we have established some level of trust. If we fail to affirm one another, or if we break the empathetic connection, then the situation will revert back to form, and the pattern we sought to break will reassert itself.

---

[56] M. Rosenberg, 2003, Op. cit., pp. 25-35.

Guessing Is Good

While the inward movement that we use in a non-violent dialogue to discern our own feelings and needs is the same (self-empathy) that we use in Focusing, a key difference is that we need also to elicit the other person's feelings and needs. Eliciting another's feelings and needs in a conflict situation is hard to do. In Focusing, my understanding is that guessing is discouraged. In NVC dialogue, guessing is encouraged. In fact, it often is the only way to move the dialogue forward so that we may acquire an understanding of the other's needs.

Letting the Solution Come

When a felt sense comes, it moves the whole situation forward. By whole I mean the solution will meet our own and the other person's needs. This is what I meant when I said I wanted to bring our discussion to a point of understanding that

A fully non-violent solution to a conflict situation arises when a felt sense forms in that situation.

The felt sense forms out of our (and the other person's) expressed needs. When a felt sense forms we feel a shift in a bodily way. The felt sense forms out of our on-going implying, and

Our implying already includes a sense of the other person, and the other person's needs that will move the situation forward.[57]

If a felt sense "gels" for us and we feel a felt shift, there is no mistaking the moment. It is a Yes! Yes! Moment, and we are unlikely to have to convince the other person of the solution. The other person will already "know" that a solution is at hand. He or she will have felt a bodily resonance of the shift in his or her own implying of the situation.[58]

---

[57] I think it is important to understand why a felt sense needs to form for only one person in a conflict situation. It is precisely because a felt sense includes a sense of the other person and his, or her needs.

[58] In the context of AVP, this is the Transforming Moment.

Making Requests[59]

Even when we "have" a solution to our needs we still have to "work it out," generally by making requests of each other. I find NVC's suggestions on how to make our requests (as positive doable requests) enormously helpful.[60] We can screw up the back end of a dialogue in the same way that we can screw up the front end by reverting to language patterns (demand language patterns) that likely got us into the conflict in the first place.

Incremental Change

I have set out this discussion of NVC dialogue in a linear form. In practice, an NVC dialogue usually is non-linear. You may, for example, have reflected the other person's feelings and needs (to your satisfaction), only to have the other respond by saying, "No, that is not what I meant. It is not what I meant at all!" and so you start the feelings/needs process over again. Or, you may have proceeded so far as to make a request based on your expressed needs, only to receive a "No!" in response, and you have to back up, pick up the process and move forward again.

Besides this back and forth within the dialogue process, I think (from my own experience) that we are more likely to find incremental changes over time in conflict situations as a felt sense forms and reforms over a series of interactions rather than one curl-your-toes moment in a single interaction.[61] We also encounter situations where no felt sense forms. In some of these situations we get what I call "partial solutions." These are solutions that form "within the situation," but still allow us to move forward by partially fulfilling our needs (and the other's needs) in the situation. Alternatively, we may find ourselves with no solution and encounter pain and suffering for our efforts to communicate. When we reveal our feelings and needs in a situation, we make ourselves vulnerable, especially in long-standing personal relationships. What we

---

[59] Ibid., 67-89.

[60] The suggested form is "Would you be willing to…?" See p. 52.

[61] E. Gendlin, APM, pp. 229-230.

say (as the lawyers say) "can be used against us." NVC dialogue, or any non-violent dialogue, is not a risk-free proposition. You need, as we tell our workshop inmate participants, "to be willing to suffer for what is important."

Speaking more broadly, the types of change in a person or a conflict situation that I have seen with non-violence are similar to those seen with any activity where a felt sense forms.[62] I see incremental changes as a person "works through" a situation. Once a person has experienced change, however, the situation is different. *Change is a revelatory experience.* Once a person has experienced change, then he or she comes back again and again for "more" change. I often ask our new inmate facilitators how they know that non-violence works. An answer that comes to my mind from one of our facilitator-training workshops was an inmate saying, "Because it lifts a great burden from my shoulders."

Any Symboling Sequence

So far I have talked about non-violence in situations where there is no direct violent confrontation. I have no personal direct experience with a felt sense forming in a violent confrontation. What I am going to say comes from what I have learned from working with inmates in our prison workshops about how a felt sense *may* form in a violent situation. Almost all the inmates we work with at NSP are violent offenders. The average sentence is twenty years. In any group of twenty inmates in a workshop some men will have killed one or more people. The men have lived, and still do live, on the edge of violence in the prison yard.

The core of our workshops is to do role-playing of conflict situations, seeking non-violent solutions in the role-play. Occasionally, when the participants get into a role-play, it may skirt on the edge of violence. This may happen, for example, when one participant puts his hands on another. We cut the role-play when we feel it is "on the edge."

I want to talk about one of these on-the-edge role-plays. This particular role-play involved a scenario based on a conflict in one of the

---

[62] For the types of changes, see H. Rice, 2007, Op. cit., pp. 10-12.

prison garden plots. At that time at NSP some inmates were allowed small garden plots where they could grow vegetables and flowers.[63] The inmates valued both the plots and their produce. This conflict scenario involved the "owner" of garden plot and his buddy coming upon another fellow and a buddy taking vegetables from the plot. A fifth fellow was a bystander. The role-play conflict escalated quickly with yelling until all four fellows were knotted together, and the bystander was standing close by. We had a hands-on situation and my co-facilitator and I were just about to cut the action, when the bystander suddenly dropped to his knees saying, "I'm having a heart attack!" He then slumped to the floor. The action stopped and everyone was absolutely still. Two of the role-play fellows gingerly approached the inmate on the floor, and asked him if he was OK. The fellow then let out a big booming laugh, and kept laughing. At first no one did anything, then the role-play guys started laughing. Soon the whole room was laughing.

In debriefing the role-pay I think that we decided the "heart attack" was a Transforming Moment. I certainly can say that it "paused" the situation. More to the point, in debriefing when we asked the bystander why he did it, he said it just came to him. He said he felt the situation was getting out of hand, and he wanted to stop the escalation. He indicated an inner voice had said, "Pretend to have a heart attack," and he just did it. We asked repeatedly if he had planned the action, until we were convinced that he had not. He said he had no idea how the "heart attack" would play out.

In retrospect, I now think a felt sense formed for him in that situation. I think the felt sense was simply a next step, "Pretend to have a heart attack."

I am telling this story to make the point that I think a felt sense can form in any situation, in any symboling sequence (pattern of words and actions). Our implying is always with us. We can turn to interact with our implying at any moment, and let a felt sense form. A felt sense forms as it

---

[63] The garden privilege has been taken away.

can form. I say this (to myself) as a reminder not to get too enamored with the steps in non-violent dialogue.

NVC Is a New Pattern

I want to make a related point by saying that the new practices, like NVC, which we are learning, are themselves new symboling sequences (patterns). We still live in symbol space, and we still live by acquiring and using patterns of words and actions. So we are fully capable of unthinkingly using NVC and other non-violent patterns as we would use any other pattern. Here, I am thinking of a conversation that I overheard at an NVC training session. I heard a young woman say to another young woman,

"I did observations/feelings/needs/and requests. I know I did it *perfectly*. I mean *just perfectly*. And nothing happened!"

We can end up *doing* the pattern, and completely miss the situation we are in. We can do observations/ feelings/ needs/ and requests, for example, when only empathy, listening, and reflecting may be required to change the situation. Or, the situation may just need something like "pretending to have a heart attack."

Cultural Transformation[64]

We usually think of our interactions as mostly private affairs. However, our interactions are not lost. What we call culture and language form in each interaction. When a felt sense (a Direct Referent) forms in an interaction, it is an entirely new (singular) event. When we think and act from that Direct Referent we form new ways (patterns) of thinking, speaking and acting. In this sense, a Direct Referent is what Gendlin calls a Universal. There is enormous transformational power in each new Universal to change how people think and act as the new patterns resonate with their own implying. I think both Focusing and NVC are new Universals. I can see both culture and language forming, deepening, and broadening around each practice (pattern). Look closely at how you now think and talk in your own group. Both Focusing and

---

[64] E. Gendlin, APM, p. 259.

NVC are growing. I think you can see, if you have not done so already, the cultural change that is occurring with and around your own practice.

Transforming Moment

I want to speak to the same point of cultural transformation by retelling an event, which happened in the non-violent Civil Rights Movement in the South in early 1960. The sequence that I am retelling was a confrontation on the Nashville City Hall steps between Diane Nash, a student leader in the Nashville sit-ins, and Mayor West, the Mayor of Nashville at the time. The event was recorded on news videotape and forms part of larger documentary piece in the PBS documentary called *A Force More Powerful*. I first learned of the sequence by watching the documentary piece. The scene has stayed (hauntingly) with me. I think it was a Transforming Moment. I am retelling the scene from the text accompanying the documentary.[65]

The Nashville sit-ins were one of the first large scale non-violent direct actions attempting to desegregate lunch counters in department stores in the South. The non-violent tactic used was to have pairs of black students sit in at the lunch counters, asking to be served. Many of the student protesters were beaten and jailed. Eventually the white establishment responded by closing the lunch counters. The non-violent leaders countered this action by mobilizing the black community to boycott the downtown department stores. The boycott was successful and had put financial pressure on the department store owners. The leaders next move was to organize a non-violent, silent march on City Hall, further escalating their demand that desegregation begin. The march mobilized all the student protesters and almost the entire black community. As the march formed, the marchers had only a promise from Mayor West that he would meet them on the steps of City Hall.

Diane Nash was among the student leaders in the vanguard of the march. The march proceeded to City Hall and up the steps at City Hall.

---

[65] The quotes are from archival news footage from Steve York's PBS documentary television series *A Force More Powerful* released in 1999, and quoted in Peter Ackerman and Jack Duvall, 2000, *A Force More Powerful*, Palgrave, New York, pp. 326-327.

Mayor West was there along with some other men. Diane Nash found herself in front of Mayor West. No one knew what to say because neither side had fully planned what would happen at this point. The dialogue that follows is the exchange between Diane Nash and Mayor West.

Diane Nash began by asking the Mayor, "Do you feel that it is wrong to discriminate against a person solely on the basis of his race and color?"

After some time the Mayor responded, "I do not agree that it is morally right to sell someone merchandise and refuse them service."

Then Diane Nash asked him, "Do you think the lunch counters should be desegregated?"

The Mayor hesitated, and did not answer.

Diane Nash asked again, "Then, Mayor, do you recommend that the lunch counters be desegregated?"

West finally said, "Yes."

The crowd cheered and the marchers congratulated one another.

This dialogue exchange was the turning point in desegregating the Nashville lunch counters, and led to the later desegregation of other public places in Nashville. The Nashville experience, in turn, led into and joined a larger pattern of sit-ins, boycotts, and marches that was repeated successfully in other cities, helping to end public segregation in the South.

When such a cultural change takes place, we say that we have had "a change of heart." Mayor West had a change of heart when he said, "Yes" to public desegregation. The city of Nashville had a change of heart when it said, "Yes" to public desegregation, and the whole of the nation eventually said, "Yes" to public desegregation. When we enter into a situation and a Transforming Moment occurs, we create a new system of possibilities for change that did not necessarily enter into the event. The process schematic (form) for change, which we are following here, is that a felt sense formed in implicit space applies to *everything*. Implicit space is a far more intricate ordering of our living. When a change occurs as we work out the instances implicit in a formed felt sense, then that change may cascade into a series of interactions (events) as others "take the change to heart." As we take the change to heart, we work out a more intricate and cooperative ordering of our lives. We experience not only our own personal change, but we also experience the cascade of change as our group, prison yard, community (or city, or nation-state) works out this reordering, as a "No" becomes a "Yes."

Ending

With the retelling of this Nashville story (above), I realized that I am at or near the end of these Notes. When I went inside to "touch" my leading, my Direct Referent, I found that the "birth" in my last Meditation was ending. There is always more, but my sense now is that the "birthing" process of these Notes is coming to an end.

Before ending, I want to comment on my intent in writing these Notes. I wanted, as I said, to provide my understanding of how we change and transform our lives.

Looking back, these Notes began with my discomfort and discontent with my own life, and my own life-understanding. I sought change and transformation by turning inward in my Quaker Meditations to wait, as we say, "in the light." What came to me, the "truth" that came to me as a way forward, was to map "old into new." That was a Transforming Moment for me. As I have said, I came alive with just that phase of mapping "old into new." I felt freedom and a release, as if I were unbound, and a surge of energy came to me in that Meditation, and the Meditations that followed, to sustain the unfolding of these Notes. This unfolding came as a language process, both in understanding how change occurs, and in the writing of these Notes. The writing shaped my understanding.

I think my felt experiencing of the language leading to my own change is part of a larger collective pattern. I think we all start (where I started) with a discomfort, discontent, or despair at our own living. We live in symbol space, in a world that we have created with language. I think that we have "filled up" this space. The roles that we have learned as language patterns no longer work for us; our living in symbol space has become too complex, or too broken, for us to carry our lives forward in any meaningful way. We experience our living as "thinned" out, emotionally flat, or "slotted" into situations where we experience a disconnect between what we feel and what we think we "should" feel and say.

As we grow older, we endure, we measure out our life... *we measure out our life with coffee spoons*. As time runs on, we become afraid, and yet more afraid that we can't change our life in any fundamental way. We find ourselves trapped within our life situations, bound by our own words and actions, which fail to carry us forward. Then, at some moment, at some still moment we turn inward, and ask in some way, "How can I change my life?" When we turn in this way, we interact with our own implying to change, and change "comes" to us. We bring our implying into our awareness, and life comes to us. We "get beyond words," we get beyond our situation. We experience life anew; life flows in and through us in an adult full-bodied way. We have a new reference outside our situation; we have a clear sense of meaning and direction. For a fortunate few, this act of turning is a natural turning. For most us, we need to learn how to turn in this way. First, we need to learn how to turn, and then we need to practice.

It was my own experience with this turning and questioning in Quaker, Focusing, and NVC practices, which shaped my understanding that we have a common language pattern in each practice. This turning and questioning is where we start in symbol space. It is "how we learn to use words to get beyond words." When we turn inward, we learn to hold a situation in symbol space, and let a felt sense form in implicit space. Our "holding and letting," or "pausing and letting," is how we learn to interact with our own implying. We "get beyond words" by turning our attention to, and letting our implying come into our awareness. Central to understanding our living as a process is the understanding that we live by implying our own change, we live into our own change. When we interact with our implying, we experience our living as a touching, or an entering into the "stream of life;" and when we make our implying explicit by symbolizing our implying, we emerge renewed and refreshed, as if we had bathed in life itself. We emerge with a new center, a formed felt sense, which shows us a next step forward, and leads us to change and transform our lives, to "speak and act" in new and life-giving ways.

Once we have experienced change, we return again and again to practice, to seek more change. We practice with those who taught us, or we seek out others who also are "seekers." We affirm, support and care for one another with empathy, listening, and reflection. When we change together in a group, we light up the whole room as we slowly and lovingly weave our way amongst each other with hugs and tears of joy. As we connect with our own change, and with one another, we are creating and being shaped by a new space – implicit space. When we create and are shaped by implicit space, we are participants in an evolution of human awareness of our own implying. Again, speaking in this larger collective sense, each of our practices, our Quaker, Focusing, and NVC practice, is an experiment in forming and extending a new language pattern, a new way of speaking and acting. As we work out our own felt experiencing of change, we are embedding our new language patterns into the mesh of countless patterns that make up symbol space, our everyday space. We are embedding the seeds for further change.

With this understanding, I hope that I have shown that in each of our practices we learn and teach how to

Use words to get beyond words in order to speak (use) words in a new way.

I also hope that we share more with each other about our separate practices so that we can deepen our understanding of what we mean when we say that we speak and act in new ways. I hope that we can help one another to bring about a deeper and wider way of living peaceably in this world.

Quaker Advice

I want to end by coming full circle and offering some old (now new) Quaker words of advice,

If you seek to change and transform your life, then turn to the inward light. Open your heart to the truth. Wait patiently in the light. Welcome the truth that comes to you. Live the truth. In living the truth you will enliven your own life, and the lives of all around you. You will enliven the world.

References

AVP/USA (2002), *Alternatives to Violence Project Basic Course Manual*. AVP Distribution Service, St. Paul, MN.

Ambler, Rex (2002). *Light to live by*. Quaker Books, London.

Ambler, Rex (2001). *Truth of the Heart*. Quaker Books, London.

Cornell, Ann Weiser (2005). *The Radical Acceptance of Everything*. Calluna Press, Berkeley, CA.

Gendlin, Eugene (1964). "A Theory of Personality Change." In *Personality Change*, Phillip Worchel & Donn Byrne (Eds.). John Wiley & Sons, New York.

Gendlin, Eugene (1981). *Focusing*. (2nd Edition), Bantam Books, New York.

Gendlin, Eugene (1991), "Thinking Beyond Patterns." In *The Presence of Feeling in Thought*, B. den Ouden and M. Moen (Eds.). Peter Lang, New York.

Gendlin, Eugene (1997). *Experiencing and the Creation of Meaning*. Northwestern University Press, Evanston, IL. [ECM]

Gendlin, Eugene (1997). *A Process Model*. The Focusing Institute, www.focusing.org. [APM]

Gendlin, Eugene and Hendricks, Mary (2004), "Thinking at the Edge: A New Philosophical Practice." In *The Folio, A Journal for Focusing and Experiential Therapy, Vol. 19, No. 1*, pp. 1-24. [TAE]

Purton, Campbell (2004), *Person-Centred Therapy*. Palgrave Macmillan, New York.

Rice, Harbert (2007), *Review Report on AVP Workshops at Nevada State Prison (NSP)*, available at www.renofriends.org/avp.

Rosenberg, Marshall (2003). *Nonviolent Communication.* (2nd Edition), Puddle Dancer Press, Encinitas, CA.

Whitmire, Catherine (2001), *Plain Living.* Sorin Books, Notre Dame, IN.

Appendices

Appendix A - Light Meditation[1]

As you have done in our previous Meditations, please choose whether you wish to meditate with your eyes open, or your eyes shut. Do whatever is natural for you when you meditate. Let's begin.

[Take five to six minutes per step.]

1. **Make yourself comfortable. Relax. Let yourself settle into silence.** Take your time to begin letting awareness come into your body … … … Let your awareness come inward, into the whole inner area of your body … into the whole area that includes your throat, your chest, your belly … … … Just be there, remembering that you have an inner knowing, an inner sense of what feels right … … … Let your awareness rest gently in that whole middle area … … … **Let yourself become wholly aware.**

2. **Now, turn towards whatever in your awareness wants your attention** … … … Sense what comes when you say, "What is really going on in my life?" Or, "What in my personal life wants my attention now?" [Or, if you have a specific question that you want to focus on, ask yourself that question now.] … … … Let the real concerns of your life slowly emerge … … … **Let the inward light show you these concerns** … … … Be still, cool, and patient.

3. **Take some time to focus on one thing that presents itself** … … … One thing that wants your attention … … … Try to get a feeling-sense of this thing as a whole … … … Try to sense the whole of this thing … … … Keep a little distance so that you can feel and sense it clearly.

---

[1] Adapted from R. Ambler, 2002, *Light to live by*.

When you are ready, try to describe this thing … … … Let a word or an image come that says what it is really like … … … this thing that concerns you… … … Let a word, phrase, or image come out of your feeling-sense of the whole of this thing… … … Let a word or image come that fits it best … … … Sit patiently with this thing that wants your awareness… … … that resonates… … … … as if you were sitting with a new friend.

4. **Now, try to sense what this thing wants you to know** … … … Don't try to explain it… … … Just wait in the light until you can sense what this thing wants you to know… … … Or, you might try to sense what this thing needs… … … As if you were asking, "What does it need?" … … … Let the answer come… … … Let the truth reveal itself… … … **Wait patiently in the light** … … … **Let the truth come.**

5. **When the truth comes, welcome it** … … … If it is the truth, you will recognize it immediately… … … You may feel the answer as a shift in your body … … …You will realize the truth is something you need to know… … …**Trust the light** … … … **Say "yes" to the truth** … … … Accept it… … … Stay with the truth for a while, it will begin to heal you.

6. **Now, consider how you need to act** … … … You will know in your heart what your response will be … … … It may be what you have been doing… … … Or it may be a new step… … … You can take the next step with certainty … … … Consider what small step you might take … … … **Let the truth show you the way forward.**

If none of this seems to have happened yet, do not worry… … … This process may take longer… … … Notice how far you have come this time, and pick up the process again on another occasion.

[Bell.] When you feel ready, open your eyes if they were closed. Stretch your limbs and bring your Meditation to an end. Please be silent.

Appendix B - Five Steps In TAE[2]

The following theory construction looks at Nonviolent Communication (NVC) from *A Process Model* standpoint and uses the first five steps from Thinking at the Edge (TAE). The theory utilizes the basic concept of "occurring into implying" from *A Process Model* (APM).[3] In the context used here, "occurring" means speaking "into implying."

The initial TAE work was done at a workshop on "Speaking from the Felt Sense" at a Focusing Institute Summer School.[4] TAE begins with a felt sense of "knowing," a sense of something I know, which I have not been able to say.

Step One – Choose something you know and cannot yet say, which wants to be said, and write a rough sentence from your felt sense of it.

The "knowing" that I want to work with is that a felt sense and felt shift occur both in NVC and in Focusing. This knowing also includes a vague sense that I can "cross" NVC and Focusing through terms from APM in a way that will deepen our understanding of both processes. The feeling quality for this knowing is an "insistence;" it has a take-me-now quality of wanting to come out.

Write down one instance of this knowing – a situation where it actually happened.

---

[2] E. Gendlin and M. Hendricks, 2004, "Thinking at the Edge: A New Philosophical Practice." In *The Folio, A Journal for Focusing and Experiential Therapy*, Vol. 19, No. 1, pp. 1-24. (TAE). Steps 1-5 are called "Speaking from the Felt Sense."

[3] E. Gendlin, 1997, APM. See p. 90 for a discussion of "occurring into implying."

[4] Given by Nada Lou in August 2006. Steps 1-5 are my notes from the TAE workshop.

The instance that I used came during an empathy session in an NVC workshop. The form for an NVC empathy session is quite similar to a Focusing session. Participants pair up and offer empathy (listening, reflecting, and gentle questioning) to one another as each, in turn, works through a conflict situation using the NVC model to make an observation of the situation, sense and express his or her feelings and needs, and to make a request based on the expressed need. This situation was the first instance where I had a "knowing" that feelings and needs are bodily sensed and that a felt sense and a felt shift occurs in the NVC process.[5]

Write down one short sentence. Underline the key word or phrase in the sentence.

In NVC, understanding that feelings/needs are an aspect of the implicit <u>allows</u> a felt sense of the situation to form.

In this sentence on NVC, "understanding" means my sense of and my understanding of NVC now allows me to facilitate/ guide/ see feelings and needs as aspects of letting a felt sense form. "Allowing" is the key word.

What allows the felt sense to form? A felt sense forms as it can form. What is new here is an understanding that a felt sense can (and does) form in the NVC process. This change in viewing NVC as a felt experiencing process leads to the understanding that feelings/needs are "<u>handles</u>" of a felt sense forming. Sensing and expressing feelings and needs perform the same function in NVC that felt sensing and expressing does in Focusing. They are aspects of symbolizing (making explicit) an implying in the situation. The formed felt sense is what will carry forward as a next step in the situation. In a conflict situation, a formed felt sense is what can change and resolve the conflict.

Step Two – Find out what is more than logical in the felt sense. Write an illogical sentence or paradox.

What is more than logical in the felt sense: Forming/ Unfolding, and Seeking/ Allowing.

---

[5] This is the NVC empathy session, which I describe on pp. 63-65.

Step Three – Notice that you don't mean the standard definition of the words. Write dictionary definitions of the key word. Use a ... for the felt sense and let a second word come, repeat finding dictionary references for the second word. Again, use ... for the felt sense and let a third word come. Find dictionary references for the third word. Repeat for a fourth word.

Allows

to let do or happen
permit
permit the presence of
permit to have
make provision for
assign

Facilitates

to make easy or easier
to make less difficult
to assist the progress of
helping bring about the
the likelihood, strength, or
 effectiveness of
be of use

Makes More Open

not closed
permit passage
having no means of
 or barring
interior immediately
 accessible
free of obstructions
without cover or
 enclosure
accessible

Makes Expressible

to put thought into words
to show, manifest, reveal
to set forth the feelings, opinions
to represent
explicit

When I worked through each set of dictionary definitions by trying each definition out as a "fit" with my felt sense, almost all the definitions "glanced off" my felt sense. They didn't "fit;" they felt "not quite right." One or two words, like "explicit" and "accessible" came close to fitting, and I had a sense of "maybe" for these words.

Step Four – Return to your felt sense and say what you wanted each of the words to mean. Underline the words that best fit your felt sense.

Write a sentence or a fresh phase to say what you wanted each of the four words to mean.

Allows

<u>lets more easily</u>
lets more awareingly
lets more freely
lets do its own thing
let do

Facilitates

makes easier
greases
smoothes the way
makes more accessible
makes alive
makes human
to make easy, easier
<u>simplifies</u>

Makes More Open

frees up
expands the opening
helps unfolding
opens to possibilities
makes for trusting
<u>more accessible</u>

Makes Expressible

makes comprehensible
make teachable
makes shareable
connectable
heartfelt
<u>explicit</u>

In NVC, understanding that feelings/needs are aspects of an implying <u>lets</u> a felt sense of the situation form <u>more easily</u>.

Understanding that feelings/needs are aspects of an implying <u>makes</u> a felt sense more accessible in NVC.

Understanding that feelings/needs are aspects of an implying <u>simplifies</u> the NVC process.

In NVC, understanding that feelings/needs are aspects of an implying <u>makes</u> forming a felt sense <u>more open</u>.

Understanding that feelings/needs are aspects of an implying <u>makes</u> forming a felt sense more <u>expressible</u> in NVC.

Step Five — Write a new expanded sentence using the key words or phrases from Step Four.

Understanding that feelings/needs are aspects of an implying <u>lets</u> a felt sense form <u>more easily/ accessibly/ simply/ openingly/ expressibly</u> … in the NVC process.

In this new expanded sentence the "allowing" in the initial sentence has opened up to say more explicitly how our understanding that we are working with a felt experiencing process will help us in our own experiencing, or in facilitating the NVC process. This understanding <u>lets</u> a felt sense form: <u>more easily/ accessibly/ simply/ openingly/ expressibly</u>.

Index

Alternatives to Violence Project (AVP), 75
   Transforming Moment, 76, 79
   Transforming Power, 76

Basic concepts, 19
   Behavior space, 24
   Eveying and crossing, 21
   Experiencing, 20
   Explication, 32
   Expression, 28
   Focaling, 22
   How words work, 36
   Interaction contexts (Situations), 24
   Life carrying forward, 21
   Metaphor, 37
   Occurring into implying, 20
   Recognition, 31
   Symbol space, 24
   Symbolizing meaning, 16, 30
   Time, 26

Behavior space, 24

Blocks
   In Focusing, 14
   In NVC (Jackal), 9
   In Quaker Practice, 7

Change, 16
   And transformation, 51-101
   Any symbolizing sequence, 93
   Incremental, 92

Complexity (in roles), 43

Crossing, 21
   In metaphor, 38
   NVC and Focusing, 107

Culture
   And language, 25
   Transformation, 95

Dialogue (in NVC), 52, 88
   Empathy first, 89
   Feelings and needs, 90
   Guessing is good, 91
   Letting solution come, 91
   Making requests, 92
   Observing without evaluating, 90
   Pausing in, 88
   Seeking common ground, 90

Direct Referent, 61

Empathy, 63
   Exercise, 83
   First in dialogue, 89

Ending, 98-101

Exercises
   Empathy, 83
   Experiment with meaning, 33
   Hard to hear messages, 86
   Illusion of conflicting needs, 84

Eveying and crossing, 21

Experiencing, 20
Explication, 32
Expression, 28

Felt meaning, 30
   Experiment with, 33
Felt sense, 16
   As Direct Referent, 61
   Forming in Meditation, 60
   In TAE, 109 (Appendix B)
   Using NVC exercises for, 83
Felt shift, 16
Focaling, 22
   Illusion of conflicting needs, 84
Focusing, 11-15
   And Light Meditation, 59
   As a skill, 14
   Blocks, 14
   Change in, 16
   Felt sense, 16
   Felt shift, 16
   Inner movement, 13
   Language sequence, 52
   Symbolizing meaning, 16

Getting beyond words, 65

Hard to hear messages, 86

Holding and letting, 70

How words work, 36

Implicit space, 65-69
   Getting beyond words, 65
   Holdings and letting, 70
   Leadings, 66

Pausing and letting, 88
   Speaking in a new way, 68
Incremental change, 92
Introduction to Notes, 1-3
   How to read, 2
   Intent and Hope, 3
   Using words, 1
Interacting with implying, 53
Interaction contexts
   (Situations), 24

Jackal Talk, 9

Language, 10
   And culture, 25
   Experiment with, 33
   Explication, 32
   Expression, 28
   How words work, 36
   Metaphor, 37
   Recognition, 31
   Sequences (Patterns), 52
   Symbolizing meaning, 16, 30
Leadings, 66
   As Direct Referent, 67
Light and truth, 71
Light Meditation, 53-58
   And Focusing, 59
   And self-empathy (NVC), 62
   Text, 107 (Appendix A)
Life carrying forward, 21
Living in symbol space, 41-49
   Always within situation, 48
   Quaker query, 49

Role complexity, 43
Slotted feelings, 41
Structure-bound, 45
Thinned living, 46

Metaphor, 37

My experience, 59
Forming a felt sense, 60
With Direct Referent, 61
With leadings, 66
With light and truth, 71
With speaking in a new way, 68

Nonviolent Communication (NVC), 8-10, 78
As a new pattern, 95
Blocks (Jackal), 9
Dialogue, 52, 88
Empathy, 63
Empathy exercise, 83
Empathy first, 89
Hard to hear messages, 86
Illusion of conflicting needs, 84
Language sequence, 52
Pausing and letting, 88
Self-empathy, 62
Thinking about, 79
Understanding needs, 79
Using exercises for felt sense, 83
Violence from unmet needs, 78

Non-violence
And AVP, 75
And NVC, 78

Notions, 7

Occurring into implying, 20

Pausing and letting, 88

Prufrock, 41-48

Quaker Practice, 5-8
Advice, 101
Forming a felt sense, 60
Language sequence, 52
Leadings, 66
Light and truth, 71
Light Meditation, 53-58, 107
Modern query, 49
Notions (Blocks), 7
Understanding Fox, 72
Where we are now, 5

Recognition, 31

Re-recognition (Expression), 28

Role-playing, 93

Self-empathy, 62

Situations (Interaction contexts), 24
Always within, 48

Slotted feelings, 41

Speaking in a new way, 68

Structure-bound, 45

Symbol space, 24
Living in, 41-49
Understanding, 19-40

Symbolizing
Any sequence, 93
Meaning, 16, 30
Sequences (Patterns), 52

Thinking
  About NVC, 79
  At the Edge (TAE), 109
      (Appendix B)
  Crossing NVC and Focusing, 109
Thinned living, 46
Time, 26
Transformation
  And change, 51-101
  Cultural, 95
Turning and questioning, 51

Understanding
  Fox in a new way, 72
  Language, 10
  Needs in NVC, 79
  Symbol space, 19-40
Using NVC for felt sense, 83

Violence from unmet needs, 78

About the Author

Harbert Rice is a Quaker, a member of the Reno Friends Meeting (Reno, NV). At various times, he has been Clerk of the Meeting, Clerk of Ministry, and Recording Clerk. He also has taught and led Light Meditation in the Reno Meeting. For the last ten years he has done volunteer service. First, he served as a hospice volunteer. And, for the last five years he has facilitated Alternatives to Violence Project (AVP) workshops in the Nevada prison system. AVP is an experiential non-violence program, which originated with Quaker work in the New York prison system. The AVP work at the Nevada State Prison (NSP) is described on the Reno Friends website at http://www.renofriends.org/avp.html. You can reach Harbert at hvrice@gmail.com.

How To Get Books

You can acquire copies of *Language Process Notes* from The Focusing Institute. To order copies, call or visit the Institute's website:

**The Focusing Institute
34 East Lane
Spring Valley, NY 10977
845. 362. 5222
info@focusing.org
www.focusing.org**